HOW TO WRITE AN AMAZING

IT

RESUME

GET THE INTERVIEW EVERY TIME

BizBooks Publishing

How to Write an Amazing Resume: Get the Interview Every Time
by Baron Fendler published By Bizbooks Publishing.

© 2017 Fendler Technologies, Inc.

Library of Congress Control Number: 2017912787

ISBN: 978-0-9993158-0-4
ISBN: 978-0-9993158-1-1 (ebook)

Cover design by Dane Low.

1.2

Acknowledgments

Writing a book is a team effort. I would like to thank Kevin Morgan, Andrea Kennedy, and Jake DeLauro for helping me understand what recruiters and hiring managers really look for in resumes; Vera Case for both her IT perspective and excellent editing; Dane Low for his outstanding cover design; Parker Fendler for his recommendations and additional editing; and Shannon Fendler for her suggestions and support throughout the process.

Table of Contents

Introduction

S o you're an IT professional and you need to write an amazing
resume? If so, this book is for you! If you want a technical job,
such as developer, technical architect, or administrator, we've got you
covered. If you're looking for a business IT job, such as analyst,
project manager, director, or even CIO, we've got you covered.
Whether you're just getting out of school and looking for your first
job, or you're an IT veteran with twenty-five years of experience, this
book has everything you need.

First things first. Let's clear up a common misconception about the
purpose of a resume. The purpose of a resume is <u>not</u> to get you a job.
It's really not. Granted, when you write a resume, you are probably
hoping to land a job. And your resume will hopefully *lead to* a job. But
that's definitely not its purpose. The purpose of a resume is
something different.

Imagine you run a car dealership and you are trying to sell a new
car. You put together a one-page advertisement for the car. Now, no
one will really buy a car purely based on the advertisement — your ad
is really just trying to entice the customer to come into the showroom
and test drive the car. That is, the purpose of your advertisement is *to
get them to test drive the car*. Similarly, your resume is just an
advertisement. It's an advertisement to sell you! If your ad is good
enough, hopefully the customer will want to take you for a test drive.

So, what is the purpose of a resume?

The purpose of a resume is to get you an *interview*.

Yes, the purpose of a resume is to get you an *interview*. This is a critical distinction. Don't fall into the trap of thinking that your resume needs to get you a job. If you do, *your resume will be too long*. You'll fill up your resume with all kinds of garbage that won't help your case at all. You may risk getting weeded out before even getting called in for an interview. In the IT world, this is a particularly common problem. There are piles of resumes out there that are way too long and have way too much technical info.

Once you get to the interview, you'll have plenty of time to go into detail about your awesome skills and to show off your great personality. But you have to get the interview first!

Know Your Audience

When you submit your resume, it will be reviewed by three types of people. Think of each person as a hurdle. Your resume needs to clear all of the hurdles before you will get the interview. And like hurdles, if your foot hits any one of them...you know what will happen.

The first person to review your resume is the **Resume Robot**. Well, this is not actually a person at all, but a computer with resume screening software. When you apply to a larger company, this is generally the first step. Here's how it works: The employer feeds key words and phrases, such as *project manager, interface developer*, or *Java*, into the software. Then the program scans your resume, tries to figure out if you match, and returns results ranked by relevancy. The resume screeners are sophisticated enough to figure out how many years of experience you may have with a particular skill. For example, if you have Java shown on five separate jobs, and the job dates go from 2007 to 2017, the resume robot may tally 10 years of Java experience for you.

Next up is the **IT Recruiter**. The IT recruiter will review resumes that made it through the resume robot. The most important thing to know about recruiters is that *they are not IT experts*. Recruiters may have some general IT knowledge, but will not have the expertise to differentiate among multiple qualified candidates. Recruiters are also super busy and will typically spend less than one minute on your resume.

The recruiter will quickly run your resume through a mental checklist. For example, this particular job might require five years of software development experience, at least one full lifecycle implementation, and a technical degree. Do you have these things? Check. Check. Check. Then the recruiter will scan for more general attributes. Do you show career progression? Do you appear to be a team player? Is your resume professional and neatly organized? Check. Check. Check. If the recruiter likes your resume, he will typically schedule a short phone interview to learn a little more about you, and if he thinks you *stand a chance* at getting this job, you'll generally pass.

Finally, your resume will be seen by the **Hiring Manager**, the person who will be your boss when you get the job. Typically, the hiring manager starts with a stack of ten or more resumes and tries to whittle them down to schedule three onsite interviews. She may spend a full five minutes or more looking over your resume—which is an eternity when we're talking about resumes!

Since the recruiter has already approved you, the hiring manager will assume your resume meets the basic checklist. The hiring manager will zero in on your more recent jobs, read the bullet points more thoroughly, and try to understand what you really did. Whereas recruiters have a standard review process, hiring managers are much more fickle. Each is different, and they often don't even know what they're looking for. *But they'll know it when they see it.* Subconsciously, what they're looking for is a *hook*. If you're able to hook them, you'll get the interview almost every time.

Win Them Over

To get over these three hurdles, your resume must do three things:

1. **Contain key words peppered throughout.** When the resume robot scans your resume, if you don't have the required key words, then it's over before it's even begun. Your resume needs the required keywords, or it will be filtered out before ever being seen by a human being.

2. **Show that you meet the "checklist".** That is, the recruiter can take your resume and compare it against their checklist and check off all the boxes. In the short-term, you can't do much about your years of experience or your degree. But you can tailor your resume to show nice balance and good communication skills. Your resume should be well organized, aesthetically pleasing, and should contain exactly zero spelling/grammar errors.

3. **Generate interest and excitement in you as a candidate**. To get past the hiring manager, your resume needs some kind of hook, or several hooks. You need to make the hiring manager want to learn more about you. Your resume should be *interesting. Exciting.*

That's it. Most IT resumes do a fabulous job of #1 and #2 above. They have a ton of technical key words and would match up to a checklist a mile long. But most resumes fail miserably in #3 above. *There is just no interest and excitement.* I have talked to hiring managers who have sorted through a stack of fifty resumes and struggled to find a single candidate they were truly excited about bringing in for an interview.

If you were writing up your online dating profile, I bet you would try to make it exciting, wouldn't you? You'd probably include some hooks to grab someone's attention. But your resume? Most people feel a little weird and unnatural trying make their resume "exciting". I mean, let's face it – it's not like your prior work experience coding HMTL is the most electrifying topic. But I'll say this one more time:

You need to build interest and excitement if you want to get an interview.

This book will show you how to do just that! We'll talk about getting you over the first two hurdles, but more importantly, what IT hiring managers look for in resumes. What *they* think is interesting and exciting. We'll discuss how you can take your own personal skills and experience and present them in a way to really grab the reader, get that interview, and ultimately land that job.

How This Book is Organized

This book has three parts.

- Part One, **Getting Ready**, helps you figure out what kind of content to put on your resume. This part answers key questions such as what resume format you should use, how many pages your resume should be, what kind of information you should include on your resume.

- Part Two, **Writing Your Resume**, walks through the IT resume from top to bottom. We'll discuss your Career Summary, Skills, Professional Experience, and Education sections, and call out what you need to include to make an impact.

- Part Three, **Resumes for Specific IT Jobs**, discusses how to tailor your resume to a specific role. We cover business and technical analysts, developers, support specialists, infrastructure jobs, and IT managers. Depending on your role, you'll highlight different accomplishments and present things in a slightly different way. Most readers find it useful to read this section in its entirety, but you may wish to zero in on the one or two roles that you find applicable.

At the end of the book are the appendixes. Please make use of them! Flip to the last few pages now, and take a couple minutes to scan through the appendixes. They have some great quick-reference information that will help you find the right words and phrases. The appendixes are excellent resources to help you get over writer's block and just get some things down on paper.

A Note about Conflicting Advice

Before we get started, one quick note about the advice presented in this book. There are hundreds of resume books, and thousands of resume experts out there. And of course, none of them agree! Should I include an objective on my resume? How many pages should my resume be? What font should I use? The possibilities are overwhelming, and for every "expert" that says one thing, five more experts say the other.

I'm happy to say that in most cases, there *are* definitive answers to these kinds of questions. So in general, this book will answer those types of questions directly. In a few cases, however, the "correct" answer is still debatable. And it may be hard to determine which path will get you closer to an interview. In these instances, this book will explain both sides of the argument and make a recommendation. You may decide to follow the recommendation or deviate from it. Either way is perfectly fine – as long as you're informed and understand the trade-offs.

Just remember that the purpose of your resume is to land you an interview. If you're thinking about adding more information, always ask yourself the question, "will this get me closer to an interview?" If the answer is no, then leave it out. Use your best judgment, and you'll probably be right more times than not. Ready, set, and here we go!

Part One

Getting Ready

Chapter 1

Create Your Message

I know what you're thinking. Maybe you should just skip past this part of the book and get straight to the good stuff.

Don't do it.

Here's why: Part Two discusses *how* to write your resume. But Part One discusses *what* to include on your resume, which is probably even more important. Remember, your resume is an advertisement. If you're selling a car, you need to include the right features in your ad. If you're selling yourself, you need to include the right features too! You need the right *content*, or how you write your resume really won't make much of a difference.

Qualifications and Competencies

The content in your resume is made up of two main building blocks: *qualifications* and *competencies*.

Qualifications are your skills, experience, and education.

This part is easy. Qualifications align nicely with the sections in your resume. You have a section called *skills*, so that must be where you list your skills. It's almost impossible to forget to include them on your resume.

Competencies are *specific areas* in which you are qualified.

This is a little trickier. Let's say you're really good at doing home improvement projects. You have ten years of experience and have taken multiple classes on home improvement. You're *qualified* at home improvement.

Of course, this won't do you any good if you are applying for an IT job! You need to outline your *relevant* qualifications. You need to have the kinds of qualifications that IT recruiters and hiring managers care about. Your competencies.

There are four key competencies relevant to IT jobs: Technical, Business, Management, and Life.

Technical Competency

When you mention IT jobs, this is the first thing people think of. The technical competency encompasses your skills, experience, and education relating to technology. It includes skills such as analysis and design, system configuration, installation, and troubleshooting. No one is an expert in all technologies, but if you have strength in this competency, you would have a good understanding of both hardware and software, along with strong proficiency in specific areas. For example, you might have deep expertise in a handful of programming languages or software platforms. To achieve a high level of technical competency requires years of experience and supporting education.

Business Competency

The business competency encompasses your skills, experience, and education relating to business. This is often overlooked but is also important to almost all IT jobs. It includes general business acumen such as an understanding of accounting, finance, manufacturing, or distribution, along with expertise in specific industries such as high tech or telecom. If you have strength in this competency, you would not only understand existing processes but also be able to find opportunities for improvement. To achieve a high level of business competency also requires years of experience and supporting education.

Management Competency

The management competency encompasses your skills, experience, and education relating to management. If you are climbing the ladder into IT management, this is even *more* important than your technical competency. It includes skills such as strategic planning, budgeting, and delegating, along with project management skills such as scope management, scheduling, and issue tracking. It also includes your overall ability to lead—the ability to grow people, build teams, and get a group together to solve a common problem. If you have strength in this competency, you see the big picture but also attend to the details as necessary. This is something that you really learn by doing. To achieve a high level of management competency requires years of experience leading projects, departments, or people.

Life Competency

The life competency encompasses your skills, experience, and education relating to life in general. This competency is important to not only IT jobs, but also to just about any job at all. It includes your work habits—attributes such as dedication, professionalism, desire to learn, and accountability. It also includes your social skills, your communication ability, and attitude. If you have strength in this competency, you get your work done without supervision, are always looking for ways to contribute, and get along well with others. To achieve a high level of life competency requires a lifelong commitment to continually improving yourself.

Putting it all Together

Each role in an IT organization typically has an associated core competency. For example, if you are a developer, your core competency is usually technical. But regardless of your role, your resume should cover your qualifications across all four competencies:

	Skills	Experience	Education
Business	✓	✓	✓
Technical	✓	✓	✓
Management	✓	✓	✓
Life	✓	✓	✓

This makes your resume well-balanced. A well-balanced resume is something that *hooks* hiring managers. They will consistently put well-balanced resumes into the "pass" stack, even if they can't necessarily articulate why. So always:

Make your resume well-balanced.

You might be wondering why this makes a difference, especially for techies such as developers or database administrators. The answer is that today's business environment is more competitive than ever, and managers must get more work done with fewer and fewer people. *Hiring managers want employees who can wear more than one hat.* They want developers who have the business knowledge to fill in design gaps and project managers who can roll up their sleeves and do hands-on work. And they want everyone on their team to communicate well and get along with others.

If your resume is well-balanced, it shows that you're flexible and can perform more than one role. It also shows that you communicate well. By touching on all four competencies, you subtly hint that you hang out with both techies and non-techies. Hiring managers will (fairly or unfairly) make the assumption that you get along with everyone and are easy to work with.

Competency Profile

The four competencies can be grouped together into a *competency profile* to show how strong a candidate is in each area. Each competency is scored from 1 to 5, where 1 means you're a novice in that area, and 5 means you have exceptional ability in that area. Graphically, the competency profile can be shown as a target, with the rings representing your score in each competency. Someone who had very little ability in all four competencies would look like this:

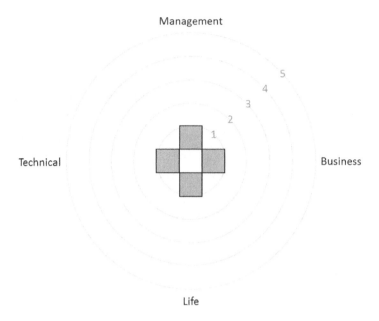

And someone with exceptional ability in all four competencies would look like this:

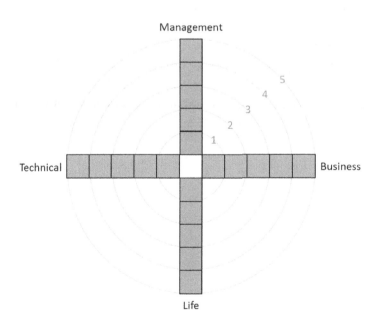

Please take a minute to review these diagrams, as we will be revisiting them throughout the book. Now, let's take Jim, a typical IT developer, as an example. He rates himself as follows:

Technical	5
Management	1
Business	1
Life	2

Jim's competency profile looks like this:

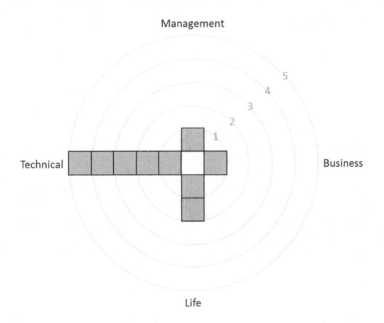

Jim is a developer, so it comes as no surprise that he has strong technical ability, and in fact, this jumps out on the diagram. But notice what else jumps out on the diagram. *In all three other competences, he is lacking.* His life competency is middle of the road – he is a hard worker and is efficient but could use more work on his social skills. His business and management skills and experience are almost nonexistent.

When Jim puts together his resume, should he highlight his strong technical skills? Absolutely! But the opportunity to make his resume really stand out is <u>not</u> going to be to in his technical competency. Hiring managers will probably already form the opinion that he is good technically. The opportunity to make his resume stand out is in the other three areas.

The opportunity to make your resume stand out is often <u>not</u> in your core competency.

Jim doesn't need to go overboard, but he should adjust his resume to give a little more focus to the other competencies. Mention some management skills. Highlight his communication ability. Use a little industry or business language in his resume. He may want to strive for something that looks more like this:

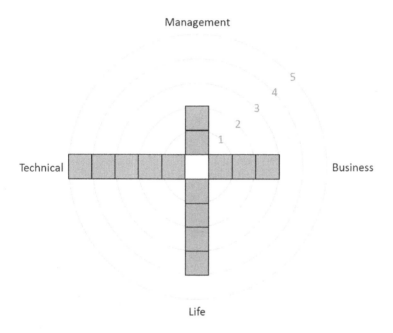

Now, while still being truthful in his resume, Jim comes across as a lot more well-rounded. A recruiter or hiring manager who picks up the resume will make more positive assumptions about him. And Jim will be more likely to get the interview.

Creating Your Competency Profile

Take a few minutes to think about your own skills, experience, and education. Perform an honest assessment of yourself. Draw your competency profile.

1) How do you rank in each of the four areas? Do you have areas that are lacking?

2) If you have an old resume, pretend you're a hiring manager. Review your resume and rank it in each of the four areas. Does your resume present you in the best possible light?

This is a five-minute activity, but for a lot of people, it is pretty sobering. What if you are weak in one or more competencies? Then it is time to start learning! Pick up a book on accounting, take an online class in project management, or sign up for a volunteer activity that requires you to present in front of people. You'd be surprised how much you can learn in a few short weeks.

Tailoring Your Competency Profile

You might be wondering if your competency profile should be tailored to your role. The short answer is yes. For example, a database administrator and an IT manager would strive for different target profiles. This is discussed more in Part Three. For now, just make an effort to touch on all four competencies.

Chapter 2

Choose Your Resume Type

M ost resume books will tell you there are three types of resumes: Chronological, Functional, and Combination. A chronological resume lists your work history in reverse-chronological order. A functional resume lists your skills in order of importance. A combination resume is (obviously) a combination of the two.

For an IT resume, choosing a type is a pretty simple. 99% of the time, you should choose the combination resume. This format is a fit for almost any candidate applying to almost any IT job. It is what recruiters expect, and it gives you the opportunity to sell yourself and not just dump information onto the reader. To repeat:

Use the combination format for your resume.

Why not use a chronological resume, the "most popular" type of resume? There are a few reasons. First, the recruiter or hiring manager must sift through your work history to try to figure out whether your experience is a fit. It's much easier to just show them up front that, in fact, you are a fit. Second, it is becoming much more common for hiring managers to use computers to screen incoming resumes. If you don't have a skills section, the resume screening software will need to try to figure out your skills, which puts you at risk of getting filtered out before ever reaching a human being. Finally, a combination resume is easier to tailor to a specific job requisition. You can make minor adjustments to your skills list, and leave everything else intact.

Resume Sections

Your resume should have five to six main sections:

1) Contact Information
2) Career Summary
3) Skills
4) Professional Experience
5) Education
6) Other Activities (Optional)

This sequence is well suited for developers and administrators all the way up to managers and vice presidents. If you are just out of school, you can expand your skills and education sections to take up more space. If you have a lot of experience, then you can stretch out your professional experience section. This sequence also effectively addresses problems such as too many short-term jobs or gaps in work history.

A Note about the Resume Objective

Once upon a time, resumes had a section called, "Objective", where you called out exactly what you were seeking. This is no longer the norm. Do not include an objective section on your resume. It takes up valuable space, and hiring managers generally skip right past them. Plus, an objective may hurt your chances of getting the interview, since you may articulate it in such a way that it doesn't seem like the right fit for the job.

Chapter 3

Design your Layout

N ext up is the overall aesthetic look of the resume. When you first pick up the resume, how does it feel? Readers will make their first judgment based simply on the feel of the resume, regardless of what the words actually say. When you take your first glance, does it feel neat and organized, or does it feel cluttered and overwhelming?

Number of Pages

The number-of-pages debate has been going on for years and continues to this day. Some recruiters and hiring managers recommend keeping your resume to one or two pages, and others don't really care if your resume is longer.

But even if only *some* of your readers prefer a resume that is two pages or shorter, isn't that *reason enough* to keep it to this length? Don't fall into the trap of thinking more is better! A longer resume may raise the concern that you have trouble summarizing and communicating information. To be safe, make your resume one to two pages.

If you have less than three years of work experience, keep it to a single page. Between three and five years of work experience, you should generally hit the two-page mark. As you gain more experience, trim your resume by removing details from older jobs.

Your most recent job might take a third of a page but a job ten years ago might have only two short bullet points.

An exception to the two-page rule could be made when you're submitting your resume to an IT agency or consulting firm. In this case, you might want to call out more detail to show that you have a very broad skillset and could be placed with many of their clients. Under this circumstance, extending your resume to three or even four pages is okay.

Font

There are many options here, and this one is easy to get anxious about. To make it simple, this book recommends going with Arial or Calibri. You can't go wrong with these. They are both sans serif fonts, which means they don't have the little decorative strokes at the ends of letters. Sans serif fonts have a modern feel, scan well, and are easy to read on mobile devices. Font guidelines:

- Use Arial or Calibri.

- Use one font throughout your resume.

- Use 14 point bold for your name at the top of the resume, and 11 point font for everything else.

- Make section headers bold and optionally in all-caps. For example, "**CAREER SUMMARY**".

- Make job titles and company names bold and regular-caps. For example, "**Peterson Manufacturing Corporation**" or "**Project Manager**".

- Bold dates. For example "**4/2014 to Present**".

- You may use a <u>single</u> additional font color in addition to regular black font. For example, you might apply a dark green or blue font wherever you use bold, which adds nice separation when your resume is viewed online.

- Don't use underlining.

This is one area where boring is good. Be simple, don't mix and match fonts, and don't get carried away.

Margins

The margins create the "shape" of the resume, which is the first thing the reader's brain will process before the reader even begins to recognize the text on the paper. Again, there are many options, but you can't go wrong with the following:

- If you don't have much experience and want to take up space, use 1 inch margins all the way around. This is pretty standard.

- If you need additional space, condense your side margins down to .75. If you still need more, condense your top and bottom down to .75.

Spacing

Be careful not to cram too much into your resume. Guidelines:

- Use single spacing.

- Apply an extra ½ space or full space to create separation between sections and jobs. Minimize use of colons and other formatters used to create separation.

- Left align all content. Do not use the "Justify Text" feature, which spreads the text evenly to the margins. Although this creates crisp margins, it also creates uneven spacing, which annoys many readers.

- Make ample use of white space. If your resume is "too texty", it is hard on the eyes.

A nicely spaced resume looks like this:

YOUR NAME

Contact Info

CAREER SUMMARY

□□
□□
□□□□□□□□□□□□□□□□□□□□□□□□□□□□□□□□□□□□□□□

SKILLS

- □□□□□□□□□□□□□   - □□□□□□□□□□□□□□□
- □□□□□□□□□□□□□□□□   - □□□□□□□□□□
- □□□□□□□□□□□□   - □□□□□□□□□□
- □□□□□□□□□□□□□□□□□□   - □□□□□□□□□□□□□
- □□□□□□□□□□□□□   - □□□□□□□□□□□
- □□□□□□□□□□□□□□□□   - □□□□□□□□□□□□□□□□

PROFESSIONAL EXPERIENCE

Company Name   **Dates**
Title

□□
□□
□□□□□□□□□□□□□□□□□□□□□□□□□□□□□

- □□□
  □□□□□□□□□□

- □□□

- □□□□□□□□□□□□□□□□□□□□□□□□□□□□□□□□□□□□□

- □□□
  □□□□□□□□□□□□□□□□□□□□□□□□□□□

- □□□

Company Name   **Dates**
Title

□□□
□□□
□□□□□□□□□□□□□□□□□□□□□

- □□□□□□□□□□□□□□□□□□□□□□□□□□□□□□□□□□□□□

- □□□

- □□

EDUCATION

□□
□□□□□□□□□□□□□□□□□□□□□□□□
□□□□□□□□□□□□□   □□□□□□□□

Notice how crisp and organized it feels. It makes a great first impression even though the resume literally doesn't say a thing.

Using Resume Templates

There are numerous resume templates available online, and you can generally download them for free. Just be aware that many of the templates out there don't meet the criteria outlined above! Some use the Times New Roman font, which was popular with printed resumes, but doesn't read well when a recruiter pulls up your resume on her tablet. Others use 10 or even 9 point fonts, which are hard on the eyes, especially for older readers. So feel free to start with a template from any of the popular resume sites, but make adjustments as necessary.

Electronic Format

We should also mention the electronic format. You will most likely create your resume using Microsoft Word or Google Docs. When your resume is complete, save it as a PDF file. Name it with your first and last name and include the word "resume". For example, "Brittany_Wright_Resume".

If you have multiple versions of your resume (and you should!), then save them in separate folders. See Chapter 11 for more information about customizing your resume for each job.

Part Two

Writing Your Resume

Chapter 4

Resume Grammar

B efore we get into the individual sections of your resume, let's cover some quick grammar lessons that you may have forgotten since middle school.

Point of View

Your resume is a short story about you. *Point of view* refers to who is telling the story. In the first-person, the writer is telling the story. For example, "I design interfaces". In the third-person, the writer is telling the story about someone else. For example, "he designs interfaces".

Write your resume in the first person. The subject ("I") is implied, so leave it out.

Some people can't stand the appearance of a fragmented sentence, so they add the subject, *I* into their resumes, as in "I developed custom reports". Yes, this is grammatically correct, but it's a horrible way to write your resume. It comes across as sounding arrogant. After reading an entire page or more filled with "I did this" and "I did that", the reader can't help but form the impression that you are full of yourself. So please leave the subject out.

Another bad option is the third person. You may have seen this before on consulting resumes. "William developed custom reports", or "Mr. Jensen developed custom reports". Don't do it. You are clearly the one writing your own resume, and when you pretend that someone else wrote it for you, it comes across as pretentious and kind of strange. I know many recruiters who *can't stand* third person resumes. Stay away from the third person.

Tense

Next up is tense. Present tense is what is happening right now. Past tense happened (and ended) in the past. Use present or past tense as follows:

- For your career summary, use the present tense. For example, in your summary, say "work effectively under high pressure".

- For your current position, if you are describing something that is *ongoing*, use the present tense. For example, "develop custom reports" or "resolve hardware problems". If you are describing something that had *a clear start and end*, however, use the past tense. For example, "upgraded department to Windows 10".

- For prior positions, use the past tense. "Developed custom reports".

Articles

You can usually eliminate *a, an,* and *the*. In resume writing, they are assumed. For example, you would say "developed application", not "developed *an* application".

Acronyms

Remember, your resume will be read by resume screening software. So you must include acronyms that might be used as part of automated search criteria, otherwise, your resume won't be picked up in the search. However, your resume will also be read by human beings, in some cases, non-technical ones, like Joe in Accounting, who doesn't know your techie jargon. Too many abbreviations, and he might not understand what you're talking about. With this in mind:

Use both the spelled out words and acronyms.

For example:
- Virtual private network (VPN)
- Search engine optimization (SEO)
- Point-of-Sale (POS)

If you use the same term multiple times throughout your resume, then use the acronym only for the second occurrence and thereafter. For example, the second time, you would just say "VPN".

This strategy generally works, but there are exceptions. Some acronyms such as SAP, IOS, and SQL are so commonly used as acronyms that most people don't even know what they stand for. Others like HTML or HTTP are too cumbersome to write out ("Hyper Text Transfer Protocol" in case you were wondering). In these cases, just use the acronym.

Numbers

In creative writing, you typically spell out small numbers. For example, in creative writing you would say *twelve* instead of 12. However, in resume writing, you should almost always use digits. This makes it easy for the reader to identify statistics and metrics at a glance.

In resume writing, use digits, even for small numbers.

For example:
- Saved $500,000 in 2 years
- Achieved 99.9% uptime
- Reduced workload by 4 hours per day

Also notice that we use the percent sign and dollar sign versus writing "percent" or "dollars". This saves space and also draws the reader's eye to the metric.

For larger numbers, write the number completely out in digits, unless it is in millions or billions. In that case, add the word "million" or "billion":
- Saved $500,000 per year
- Saved $5 million per year
- Grew company to $2 billion

Do not use M to abbreviate million, because M is also commonly used in Europe to abbreviate thousands (M is the Roman numeral for thousand). So write "$250 million", not "250M".

Note: Once in a while, you might spell out the number, but only if it is both a small number and <u>not</u> an important statistic. For example, you might say, "attended two schools", as part of your career summary. In this example, the fact that it is two schools is really just part of your background, not a notable statistic.

Chapter 5

Contact Information

T he header of your resume should include the following information:

1. Your name
2. The city and state where you live
3. A single phone number (cell phone preferred)
4. A single email address (personal email)
5. Your LinkedIn URL
6. The phrase "Open to relocation" if relevant

That's it. Do not include the word "resume". Do not include multiple phone numbers or email addresses. And no fax number. You don't need anything about Twitter or Facebook. You don't even need to label your information with words like "Phone:" or "Email:" – they'll be able to figure it out!

General Contact Info

Your name should be in large, bold print, at the top. Your city, state, phone, LinkedIn URL, and email should follow. The sequence is not important, but aim for nice symmetry. This is a good example:

David L. Morgan
Baltimore, MD | (415) 422-8015
Linkedin.com/in/DavidLMorgan
david_morgan@gmail.com

Notice, you can put multiple items on one line. Separate with a vertical line, diamond, or square (| , ◆ , or ■). The vertical line is on most keyboards, and the diamond and square can be found in Wingdings or similar fonts.

Also, notice the email address. It is simply the candidate's first and last name at Gmail. If your email is something left over from college (e.g. "crazysnowboarder@gmail.com"), then it's time to get a more professional email!

If you want your contact information to take up less space, then use a more modern format, like this:

DAVID L. MORGAN
(415) 422-8015   ◆   david_morgan@gmail.com   ◆   LinkedIn.com/in/DavidLMorgan   ◆   Baltimore, MD

These examples are pretty basic, nothing exciting. Which is perfectly okay. In fact, many hiring managers are turned off by overly stylistic headers. So in general, keep it simple.

The one exception is if you're applying for a position where creativity is a requirement of the job. In this case, you'll want to spruce it up a bit. For example, a web designer might add some style and flair, like this:

DAVID L. MORGAN
(415) 422-8015   ◆   david_morgan@gmail.com   ◆   LinkedIn.com/in/DavidLMorgan   ◆   Baltimore, MD

Don't get carried away, though. Remember, your resume will

likely be scanned by the resume robot before ever being seen by a human being. If you get too stylish, you'll risk having your name or key contact information misinterpreted by the software.

Contact information is a controversial topic, with some debate about whether you should include your physical mailing address, photo, or LinkedIn address. We'll discuss these items below.

Physical Mailing Address

Some recruiters recommend including your physical mailing address. They argue that if you leave it off, it looks like you're trying to hide the fact that you don't live locally. The reader might worry that you live in a different country and that you'll have trouble getting proper work authorization. On the other hand, including your mailing address raises privacy and identity theft concerns, especially when posting your resume online. So a reasonable compromise is to include your city and state, which is what this book recommends. This is becoming a common enough practice that it won't raise any eyebrows.

Your Photo

Photos have traditionally been excluded to protect candidates from discrimination (and employers from discrimination allegations), based on race, age, or even weight or attractiveness. In this multimedia age, the employer is likely to find your photo on social media, so the concern is admittedly somewhat outdated. But many employers and recruiters still don't think it's appropriate, and some even have blanket policies to reject resumes with photos. To be safe, this book recommends that you leave your photo off.

LinkedIn URL

Some recruiters argue that your LinkedIn URL is a distraction, and gives your employer an excuse to go surfing around on the web, rather than just calling you in for an interview. However, most recruiters recommend including your LinkedIn profile, which is what this book recommends.

LinkedIn provides a nice forum to show off your photo, without it actually being on your resume. And you should absolutely include your photo on your LinkedIn profile. Your photo shows that your profile is real (not a "spam" profile), and allows someone from a past job to easily recognize you. Have your picture professionally taken, and be sure you are dressed nicely and smiling.

LinkedIn also lets you include *recommendations*, which usually look a little out-of-place on a resume. A solid recommendation from your prior boss can put your resume straight into the "pass" stack.

Finally, make sure your LinkedIn profile parallels your resume. Your profile doesn't need to include *exactly* the same information as your resume, but your previous employers, employment dates, and general work history had better match. If they don't match, it looks like you're plagiarizing in one place or the other, which is a sure way to get eliminated as a candidate.

By the way, you can create a custom, shorter, LinkedIn URL. So if you don't like *linkedin.com/in/Jim-Jones-5a0639*, you can shorten to something easier to remember, as long as it's not already taken. If you're lucky, you'll be able to use your first and last name only. For more information, go to LinkedIn Help on the topic "Customizing your Public Profile URL".

Chapter 6

Career Summary

Alternate titles: Summary or Professional Profile

Your career summary is basically you-at-a-glance, your "elevator pitch", with a little personality. In this section, you'll write 3 - 5 sentences describing who you are, what you do, and why you're qualified. This section is critical, as many recruiters will make their decision based on these first few lines.

A good career summary shows that you are well rounded. In Chapter 1, we discussed the four key competencies: Technical, Business, Management, and Life. Your career summary should touch on at least three, or even all four competencies.

In the first sentence, define who you are and how much experience you have. For example, "Exceptional developer with 20 years of IT success." If you don't have a lot of work experience yet, you may instead call out something else significant such as a key skill. A strong opening sentence starts with an adjective. Here are some examples:

- Proven IT leader with ability to...
- Business savvy IT professional who...
- Certified systems administrator offering...
- Respected IT leader with...
- Accomplished IT professional who combines...
- Senior Java developer with a proven track record of...

- Recent college graduate with a desire to...

In the next sentence or two, call out your skills and track record, indicating your high-level accomplishments. For example, "History of building progressively more complex programs across a wide variety of clients in almost every industry." Below are some more ideas:

- Track record of...
- Background including...
- General knowledge of...combined with deep expertise....
- Proactively implement solutions that...
- Analyze ... and implement ...
- Identify... and initiate....

In the last sentence, say something about your interpersonal skills or hard work and dedication. This sentence is very deliberately focused on the life competency. For example, "Energetic, positive, and work effectively in high-pressure situations." Some other ideas:

- Team player who is always looking for ways to contribute...
- Self-starter who delivers...
- Highly motivated individual who takes initiative...
- Proactive, energetic, and get along well with others...
- Quick learner with excellent communication skills...
- Energetic team player who works hard but also...

See Appendix A for additional career summary words and phrases.

When you put it all together, a strong career summary sounds something like this:

Exceptional developer with 20 years of IT success. History of building progressively more complex programs across a wide variety of clients in almost every industry. Deep expertise in C++, Java, Visual Basic, and many other programming languages. Energetic, positive, and effective in high-pressure situations.

Sounds pretty great, doesn't it?

Let's do a quick analysis. The writer's core competency is obviously technical. He nails this with discussion on building complex programs, deep expertise, and multiple programming languages. But notice that he also mentions clients *in almost every industry*. This is a subtle hint at his business awareness. He must have encountered industry-specific requirements and coded solutions for them. A nice bump for his business competency. Finally, the entire last sentence really highlights his strength in the life competency. Overall, this sells him as a great, well-rounded candidate.

Here is another example, this one for an IT Manager:

> Proven leader with ten years of IT project management and business experience. Rapidly identify problems, initiate change, and implement new processes in challenging environments. Positive attitude and excellent communication skills. Always looking for ways to bring out the best in teams.

Another wow! The writer's core competencies are probably both management and business. We can infer that he delivers IT solutions, but he uses non-technical terms like *initiate change* and *implement new processes*. This ups his business competency, and since these types of activities require teams, the reader also picks up on his strength in the management competency. Again, we see a last sentence that highlights the life competency. Sounds like another super, well-rounded candidate.

Using Descriptive Words

Notice the use of descriptive words: Exceptional, complex, rapidly, challenging, energetic, positive, excellent.

Now, you cynics out there (you know who you are) might point out that these paragraphs are made up almost entirely of unsubstantiated claims. Just writers using a bunch of adjectives to pump themselves up and sound better.

All I can say is that it works. Descriptive words hook the reader and, in a very short amount of time, convey a positive image of you. So be descriptive. Brag a little.

Use descriptive words in your Career Summary.

But also note that *your career summary is the only place in your resume where you can get away with this type of writing.* As you move onto the other sections in your resume, you will be a little more factual and a little less opinionated.

Indirectly Stating an Objective

Earlier, we discussed that it is no longer appropriate to include an objective section in your resume. However, there are cases where you might want to *indirectly* call out an objective as part of your career summary.

Let's say you are a non-traditional candidate for a job. A long-shot. Maybe your experience is a complete mismatch for the job, but you know you would be great if you could just get your foot in the door. You might indirectly state your objective to address this concern before it is raised. What you're doing is subtly explaining why you're even applying for this position.

Below, we have a candidate applying for developer position. This candidate was previously an IT manager, so would generally be considered overqualified.

Experienced IT manager seeking to get back into hands-on development. Wealth of business and technical experience. Uncharacteristic developer who not only loves the software, but also enjoys, testing, documenting, and interacting with business users. Disciplined, thorough, and passionate about technology.

Notice what he's done here. *Seeking to get back into hands-on development*. We can immediately guess that he doesn't have as much development experience as other candidates. Rather than make the reader sift through his work history and figure this out, he addresses this fact head on. But also notice that he turns it into a strength! Some developers, as you may know, don't like doing mundane tasks such as documentation and testing. But this guy sounds like he loves that stuff! And he also has business experience and even enjoys interacting with users. He sounds easy to work with, a breath of fresh air. I'd like to hire him!

Including a Job Title

When a job becomes available, the hiring manager will create a job requisition, which calls out the job title, duties to be performed, and skills required. The requisition is usually available online, either on the job posting site or the company's own website. It gives you some great information that you can use to customize your resume to that particular job.

Always thoroughly review the job requisition before submitting your resume.

Let's say you're a programmer, and you happen to know Java and C++, along with some other languages. During your job search, you come across a job opening that you really like, look over the requisition, and notice that it says "Seeking Java / C++ Developer".

Now you might think that someone just quickly slapped this title together, but that isn't how it generally works. What is more likely is that the hiring manager met with the recruiter, they put significant thought and discussion into what the job should be called, and then *jointly determined that this is the best title for the job*. In other words, it is exactly what they are looking for.

How can you use this to your advantage?

Describe yourself *using the exact same phrase they use in the requisition* (as long as you can do so without lying). If the title they use is atypical for the IT industry, then describe yourself using a similar title that would be considered more standard. Try to match pretty closely while still being truthful.

The best place to do this is right above your career summary:

David L. Morgan

Baltimore, MD | (415) 422-8015
Linkedin.com/in/DavidLMorgan
david_morgan@gmail.com

Java and C++ Developer

Career Summary

Exceptional developer with 20 years of IT success. History of building progressively more complex programs across a wide variety of clients in almost every industry. Deep expertise in C++, Java, Visual Basic, and many other programming languages. Energetic, positive, and effective in high-pressure situations.

Notice how this reads. It reads like you are using this title to introduce yourself: David Morgan, Java and C++ Developer.

Suddenly, you sound like a *perfect* fit for the job.

This little trick works at every step in the process. You are more likely to get picked up by the resume robots because the exact job title is likely to be used as search criteria. You are more likely to pass recruiters, because remember, they'll spend less than a minute on your resume, and you've now included a flashing beacon calling out to them that you are a match for the job. Finally, this strategy even works on hiring managers, although on a more subconscious level. They will assume you are a fit for the job until proven otherwise, rather than assuming the opposite.

Chapter 7

Skills

Y our skills section is designed to get picked up by resume screening software or to catch a hiring manager's attention.

To get started, flip to Appendix B, where you'll see skills listed for each competency: Management, Business, Life, and Technical. Jot down a few skills that apply to you. Choose at least a couple from all four competencies—remember, you want to come across as well rounded. Feel free to come up with your own, too.

Regardless of your position, include both technical and non-technical skills.

For example, a developer should start with general technical skills that any IT professional would understand. Then he would follow with specific languages and techno-jargon. At the bottom, he would round it out with business, management, or life skills. A complete skills section would have 15 to 25 skills listed in two to three columns. For our developer, it might look something like this:

SKILLS

- GUI design
- XML
- IOS / Swift
- CSS
- Creative thinking

- Database design
- C++, C#
- SQL, MySQL
- Visual Studio
- Leadership

- Mobile development
- HTML, DHTML
- Java, JavaScript
- Business metrics
- Self-motivation

The reader can quickly see that this is a technical guy, but he also sounds *balanced*. Well rounded. Some skills, such as *mobile development* and *database design* are technical skills but stated in plain English. Others are techie abbreviations that really get into the nuts and bolts of this candidate's skillset. And others come from the non-technical competencies, nicely rounding out the skillset.

You may want to include one or two skills not typically associated with the job you are applying for. For example, our candidate has included *creative thinking* and *self-motivation*. These might sound a little odd, but including them helps in multiple ways. First, it shows balance. Second, it shows that the candidate has enough self-awareness to really think about and understand his or her skillset. Finally, these types of skills can be *hooks*. Maybe a particular hiring manager has been hoping to find someone to inject some creativity into her department, and she comes across this resume where the candidate specifically calls out *creative thinking* as a skill. Based on that one bullet point, this resume might go straight into the "interested" stack.

As another example, let's look at a technical analyst. A technical analyst would start with business skills, follow with technical skills, and sprinkle in some management and life skills. You would see fewer abbreviations and techno-jargon. It might look like this:

SKILLS

• Business process design	• Six Sigma
• Manufacturing strategies	• Supply chain optimization
• SAP Transportation planning	• SAP Sales order processing
• SAP configuration (SD, MM, PP)	• Enhancement design
• Data conversion	• Master data management
• Custom software development	• User training
• Team leadership	• Conflict resolution

In this example, the reader picks up a strong business competency, but also sees technical skills such as *data conversion* and *enhancement design*. We see *team leadership*, a solid management skill. Again, all competencies are represented, resulting in good balance. The oddball here might be *conflict resolution*. Although unusual, this could be a nice targeted hook for a hiring manager who might feel that his department is a little dysfunctional and in need of someone to help smooth things over.

Desktop Skills

The only time you should list desktop applications — such as Microsoft Office, Microsoft Windows, and Google Chrome — is when you are applying for a position as a support specialist. When you list these types of skills on an IT resume, you imply that you have experience not only using these applications, but also *supporting* them. That you have done installations, upgrades, troubleshooting, patching, etc.

For all other IT roles, do <u>not</u> list desktop applications as skills. The hiring manager will assume you have user-level knowledge of desktop applications, so you don't need to specifically call them out.

Telling the Truth

Adding extra skills increases your odds of getting hits on resume screening software, so you might be tempted to stretch the truth a little in this section. Maybe add a few terms you've seen on your friend's resume or some acronyms that you've read about online. **Don't do it.**

Once you make it past the initial screening, you'll typically be interviewed by four or five people — just for one job. The interviewers will each latch on to something different on your resume. They could zero in on any one of the specific skills you call out and start asking questions about it. A lot of questions. So to be safe, only include a skill if it is legitimate.

This applies to the unusual skills too. If you list something such as *conflict resolution*, be prepared to explain why your level of expertise in that skill is significant enough to justify calling it out on your resume.

Chapter 8

Professional Experience

Alternate title: Career Progression

This is the big one. The professional experience section may take up half of your resume or more. This is the section where you have the best shot at hooking the reader.

Begin with your most recent job and go in reverse chronological order, listing jobs or roles. For each role, include a Header, Overview, and Accomplishments. Each role should look like this:

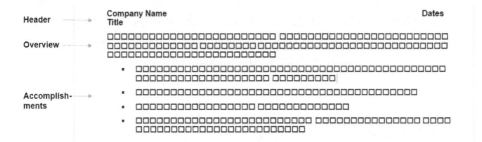

Role Header

In the role header, indicate the company name, your role or title, and the dates in which you worked there.

- **Company Name**. Use the general name of the company. You don't need to use the legal corporate name. If the company has been acquired and now has a different name from when you worked there, show the current name followed by the old name in parenthesis. For example, you would say "Accenture (formerly Andersen Consulting)".

- **Role or Title**. Call out a title that makes the most sense for your resume, as long as that title fits the tasks you performed and is *truthful*. You don't need to use the title in your official job description. For example, you might wish to take your formal title, "Manager of Business Intelligence", and shorten it to simply "IT manager".

- **Dates**. Include months and years for recent jobs. For example, "3/2012 – 9/2014" or "1/2014 – Present". If you've had a lot of short term jobs and attempt to cover it up by leaving off the months, it looks suspicious, and almost all recruiters immediately spot this. So include the months, and be prepared to address gaps in the interview. For roles five years or more into the past, it is okay to show years only.

Role Overview

In the role overview, briefly explain your role, touching on the business scope, technical scope, or both.

- **Your Role**. Describe what you did in very general terms, and for whom. For example, "developed sales and ecommerce applications for this leader in sports apparel". Mention the company's industry and its position within that industry, which highlights your business competency.

- **Business Scope**. Say something about the number of users, customers, sites or distribution centers. For example, "supported 40 sites and over 500,000 customers." If the company is international, then call out specifics about its geography. This hints at big-picture thinking and awareness.

- **Technical Scope**. Next, cover technical scope. Call out high-level details about whatever technologies you used. Mention things like databases, applications, platforms, modules, or programming languages. For example, "developed applications using Visual C++ and Java".

When you put your role overview together, it sounds like this:

Developed sales and ecommerce applications for this global leader in sports apparel. Supported 40 sites and over 500,000 customers. Applications primarily coded in Visual C++ and Java.

That's it. The role overview doesn't need to knock anyone's socks off. Its purpose is simply to demonstrate good communication skills. You give the reader some context, before diving into bullet points. Then, when the reader gets to your accomplishments, he can make some connections and better visualize and understand what you really achieved at that job.

See Part Three for more information about customizing your role overview by type of job.

Accomplishments

Next come your bullet points. This is where most IT resumes go bad. Because most IT resumes are filled with *tasks*. When you were at company XYZ, you coded, you put together test scripts, you executed tests, and so on. At the next company, you did the same thing. And at the next company. There is nothing unique, your resume starts to sound really repetitive. It is *boring*. If you focus on tasks, you will quickly run out of ways to say the same thing.

To make your resume interesting, focus instead on *projects and accomplishments*. Let me say this again:

Your bullets should call out projects and accomplishments.

Begin each bullet point with a verb. To describe what you performed directly, use hands-on verbs such as *designed, configured,* and *developed*. Whenever possible, call out improvement associated with your work. Use improvement verbs such as *attained* and *streamlined*.

Hands-on impact verbs:
- Developed
- Created
- Wrote
- Designed
- Configured
- Defined

Improvement impact verbs:
- Reduced
- Attained
- Streamlined
- Automated
- Accelerated
- Demonstrated

To describe tasks you managed, use higher-level verbs such as *managed* or *coordinated*. Or use phrases such as *accountable for* to indicate oversight over projects or activities.

Management impact verbs:
- Implemented
- Managed
- Organized
- Coordinated
- Responsible for
- Accountable for

To describe tasks you helped with, but did not legitimately perform on your own, use participation verbs, such as *assisted* or *co-developed*.

Participation impact verbs:
- Participated in
- Jointly prepared
- Co-developed
- Assisted
- Strengthened
- Learned

See Appendix C for a complete list of impact verbs.

Building a Bullet Point

Let's start with a good bullet point and make it better.

Good
- Completed e-commerce programming tasks.

Better
- Created e-commerce functionality to suggest complimentary products upon checkout.

Best
- Created e-commerce functionality to suggest complimentary products upon checkout. Project increased average order value by 16%.

Let's take a look at the progression here, from good to better to best. The first version of the bullet point outlines the task that was performed, which is what most people do in their resumes. It is okay, but as mentioned above, tasks do a poor job of generating interest.

The second version is better. *Created e-commerce functionality to suggest complimentary products upon checkout.* This version restates what you did in terms of the end result. An *accomplishment*. It is now clear that you understand and care about how your work fits into the bigger picture. Now we're not just talking about programming tasks, we're talking about suggesting complimentary products, which means *getting customers to buy more.*

This bullet point has now turned into a *hook.* Every company wants their customers to buy more! If you ask any e-commerce manager, I can guarantee you that getting customers to buy more is a topic that comes up very frequently. Probably almost every day. If I'm the e-commerce manager, and suddenly this resume lands on my desk, I am now *interested.*

The final version adds the icing to the cake. *Project increased average order value by 16%.* Now, not only do you understand the business issue, you demonstrate that you did something to improve it. You have the metric as proof! When you add it all up, this is the kind of bullet point that really grabs a hiring manager. As a hiring manager, *I'm now very interested. I want to call you in for an interview to learn more.*

Notice the final version has two sentences in one bullet point. Can you do that? Absolutely! You are conveying a lot of detail and it would be a little long to wrap the entire thought into one sentence. Also, if you read carefully, you will see that in the second sentence, the *project* increased average order value by 16%, not you all by yourself. This is perfectly okay, and is in fact more believable than trying to take sole credit for such significant improvement.

Let's go through another example.

Good
- Built enhancements to shopping cart checkout procedure.

Better
- Built enhancements to reduce shopping cart abandonment.

Best
- Built enhancements to streamline checkout process. Reduced shopping cart abandonment by 22%.

Again, let's discuss the progression here. The first version of the bullet point indicates the task performed. Not super exciting.

The second version restates this in terms of the end result. It calls out the accomplishment, the business problem that is being solved. *Built enhancements to reduce shopping cart abandonment.* This bullet point has also now turned into a hook. Anyone who works in e-commerce will immediately recognize the term "shopping cart abandonment" — when a customer fills up their shopping cart, and then at the last minute get sidetracked, and doesn't complete the transaction. Companies lose millions of dollars to shopping cart abandonment. So, you've hit a nerve with this one. As a hiring manager, *I am interested.*

The final version ups the ante. You add a minor detail about the solution, *streamline checkout process,* and hit it home with the metric: *Reduced shopping cart abandonment by 22%.* Now, as a hiring manager, I want to know more. What did you do to streamline checkout that was so effective? I might be thinking we could do the same thing at my company. *I'm now very interested. I want to call you in for an interview to learn more.*

Another example:

Good

- Coded and tested programs for point-of-sale system.

Better

- Coded and tested point-of-sale functionality to process orders and manage inventory.

Best

- Co-developed point-of-sale application that processes 25,000 transactions daily. Responsible for complex scenarios such as partial exchanges and returns.

Once again, the first version calls out the tasks that were performed.

The second version again restates this in terms of the end result. Now we're talking about processing orders and managing inventory. These are common functions in point-of-sale (POS) systems, and although the bullet isn't a strong hook yet, it is starting to generate some interest.

In the final version, you add *processes 25,000 transactions daily*. The reader infers that the solution must be robust and in use in a number of stores. In this example, we see a technical metric, transaction volume. This isn't quite as strong as the business metrics used in the prior examples, but sometimes your projects just won't have measurable business results. Did the stores sell more just because of a new POS system? Maybe not. So a technical metric is the next best thing.

Also notice the addition, *responsible for complex scenarios such as partial exchanges and returns*. This is a *targeted hook* that aims to catch a specific group of readers, in this case, those who have worked with POS systems. If you happen to be in that group, you probably know exactly what I'm talking about—returns and exchanges cause headaches in POS systems. They are the exception, not the rule, and customers somehow figure out hundreds of unique ways to return or exchange something. Here we have a candidate who has handled these before. If I'm a hiring manager who has worked with POS systems, *I'm interested.*

The majority of your readers won't get hooked by this bullet point, and that's perfectly fine. But adding targeted hooks throughout your resume adds up. It's like going fishing and cast five or six lines. You'll get them to bit on something.

Original Versus New Bullets

We started with bullets that simply described tasks performed. Below are these original bullet points:

ABC Brands   **1/2014 – Present**
Developer
- Completed e-commerce programming tasks.
- Built enhancements to shopping cart checkout procedure.
- Coded and tested programs for point-of-sale system.

Now, the new bullets. We'll add in the role overview to give our readers some context:

ABC Brands   **1/2014 – Present**
Developer
Developed sales and ecommerce applications for this global leader in sports apparel. Supported 40 sites and over 500,000 customers. Applications primarily coded in Visual C++ and Java.

- Created e-commerce functionality to suggest complimentary products upon checkout. Project increased average order value by 16%.

- Built enhancements to streamline checkout process. Reduced shopping cart abandonment by 22%.

- Co-developed point-of-sale application that processes 25,000 transactions daily. Responsible for complex scenarios such as partial exchanges and returns.

Wow! Now this candidate is *interesting*. These bullets illustrate a balanced candidate, someone who is strong across multiple competencies. A candidate who doesn't just code programs, but who understands the business problems that are being solved. Someone who delivers results. Someone who is solving *the very same problems hiring managers experience every day*.

Turning Your Bullets into Hooks

An IT manager I know recently encountered an issue resulting in significant production downtime. It was quite a fire drill – a full week of meetings running late into the evening. At 6 pm on Friday, the manager finally made it back to his desk, saw the stack of resumes the recruiter had left there, and remembered that on top of this fire drill, he still had to deal with filling an open position. Exhausted, he started to go through the resumes, one by one. Then something *interesting* happened. He picked up a resume, and this candidate had encountered and solved *the very same issue they had been chasing all week*. The manager jumped up and raced down the hall to see if the recruiter was still in the office. You can bet that candidate got the interview!

This story illustrates an important fact about hiring managers and about human beings in general: People are primarily concerned with their *own* problems. If I, as a hiring manager, pick up your resume and believe you might have a solution to my *own* problem, now you've got my attention. This is a powerful concept. You can use it to hook me in multiple ways:

1. Show that you solved a problem that my company also experiences. If you just say you built enhancements, that doesn't tell me much. But if you say, *built enhancement to handle sales compensation and third-party commissions*, it becomes a

potential hook. You've solved a business problem, one that is common to a lot of industries. It is quite possible that my company has this problem *right now*. If I brought you into my company, and you could solve the same problem here, then it would make *me* look really good.

2. Show that you solved a problem that I experience personally. If you just say you rolled out Wi-Fi routers, then that won't grab my attention. But if you add *almost completely eliminated dropped connections* to that bullet point, it turns into a strong hook. Why? Because this is a problem that I experience *personally*. In fact, dropped connections drive me crazy! This is a problem I have been experiencing for years, and it sounds like I may have finally found someone who could solve it. This would make me very happy.

3. Show that you solved a problem and have a metric to support it. Even if the specific problem isn't relevant to me, the metric gets my attention. Why? Because it shows that you improve metrics, which is something that I care about. As a hiring manager, I will conclude that *you must be able to solve other problems that I care about*. This leads me right back to #1 or #2 above. I start to think about other issues I'm dealing with right now and believe that you might be the person to solve them for me.

A word of caution about metrics. It's easy to get carried away and exaggerate, which will get you into a lot of trouble in the interview. Interviewers will ask you all kinds of questions about the claims you make—how you measured the improvement, whether you have supporting documentation, and if there is someone they could contact to verify. Only quote metrics if they are legitimate, and you are able to support them.

Task Bullet Points

Earlier, we said that in order to make your resume interesting, you should focus on projects and accomplishments, not on tasks. This is absolutely true. However, once you have loaded up on projects and accomplishments, it's okay to add a couple of task bullet points to round out the section. This is an easy way to get buzzwords into your resume that might get picked up in resume screening software. It is also a great way to show progression—calling out tasks early in your career, and accomplishments later in your career, shows that you've grown. You convey that you're no longer just doing tasks; you're now accomplishing bigger things. Examples of task bullet points:

- Coded additional programs in Visual Basic, Java, and C++.

- Prepared test cases, executed unit tests, and documented results.

- Developed user manuals and other technical documentation.

Awards and Recognition

Finally, you may also want to highlight awards, recognition, or even citations from performance evaluations. Call these out as the last bullet point beneath the applicable job. This punctuates your bullets with additional proof that you are a high performer—not only did you accomplish something, but you *were also recognized for it*. Examples:

- Received company's global award for innovation in business intelligence.

- Earned top evaluation grade 6 quarters in a row. Recognized as "superior performer who carefully weighs options before choosing a course of action".

- Promoted to senior consultant in 9 months.

Please note that you should use awards and recognition sparingly, as too much will come across as arrogant.

Chapter 9

Education

Alternate titles: Education and Training, Education and Certification.

This section lists your college degrees and any other relevant training or certifications. For schooling, show the name of the degree, graduation date, and school. For certifications, call out the name of the certification and abbreviation if applicable.

Example 1 – IT Director

If you've been out of college for several years, then this section would typically be smaller, and that's okay. An IT director, for example, has nothing to really sell or differentiate here. It is simply a matter of showing the hiring manager that you have the necessary degree or degrees. It might look like this:

EDUCATION
MBA, University of Washington, 2004
BS Accounting and Finance, University of California, Los Angeles, (UCLA) 1995

Example 2 – Recent Graduate

If you're a recent college graduate, then this section will generally take up more space. List your GPA if it is impressive and include your major if it's relevant. If you're struggling to fill up an entire page for your resume, then also list courses taken. Here is an example:

EDUCATION
BS Computer Science, UCLA, 2016, GPA 3.8

Courses taken:
- Intro to Computer Science
- Analysis and Design 1
- Programming in Java 1
- Multicore Programming
- Intro to Data Science
- Advanced Algorithms
- Analysis and Design 2
- Programming in Java 2
- Advanced Database Structures
- Practical Machine Learning

Example 3 – Technical Candidate

If you're a more technical candidate, then also include relevant certifications. If you've attended significant training courses since college, then add "Professional Training", and bullet out whatever is relevant, or to cover numerous professional courses, add a catch-all bullet at the very bottom. Example for a technical candidate:

EDUCATION AND CERTIFICATION
BS Management Information Systems, University of Arizona, 2010

Certifications:
- Microsoft Certified Systems Administrator (MCSA)
- Microsoft Certified Desktop Support Technician (MCDST)
- Microsoft Office Specialist (MOS)
- Certified Java Developer (6 week IBM Java Academy)

Professional Training:
- Attended over 16 weeks of development courses throughout career

Chapter 10

Other Activities

Alternate titles: Activities, Activities and Interests, Other Information.

This section is a great way to round out your resume, highlighting competencies you may have underrepresented. Don't just list an activity because it's something that you do regularly. *Use this section strategically.* If you don't have a lot of work experience, add activities that highlight your technical skills. If, conversely, your resume feels a little too technical, then add activities that call out your business or interpersonal talents. Remember, the opportunity to make your resume stand out is often not in your core competency.

Many recruiters will tell you to include only relevant information here. That's true, but you need to greatly expand your definition of "relevant". Include anything that highlights a skill *that is transferrable into the workplace.* List activities, for example, that show leadership, dedication, initiative, mentoring, teamwork, communication, interpersonal skills, or strategic thinking.

Non-technical Activities

You may not think that running marathons would be relevant. But this activity demonstrates hard work and dedication to achieve a goal. That's pertinent to just about any job! How about coaching a Little

League team? Coaching requires leadership, analysis, and teamwork. Maybe you volunteer to teach kids to read. Patience, mentoring, and a willingness to put in extra hours. The list goes on and on. When you do other activities, you practice a number of skills that are applicable to your job.

Include any of the following types of non-technical activities:
- A board or committee that you lead or have a seat on
- Any kind of organization you are involved with
- Teaching or training just about anything
- Volunteering or giving back to the community
- Coaching a team
- Playing a sport competitively
- Anything in which you have achieved a level of mastery
- An activity that requires public speaking or presentation
- Blogging, writing, or authoring books or articles
- Being fluent in a foreign language

Technical Activities

If you're just out of school and don't have a lot of work experience, this section is also a great opportunity to call attention to your technical skills. Do you participate in an open source development? Do you have side projects on GitHub? These types of things show that you are building technical skills, even if you don't have years of professional experience. Plus, you paint the picture that you work because you want to, not because you have to—a very positive message to send to a potential employer.

Include these types of technical activities:
- Coding as part of open source development
- Participation of any kind in open source projects (testing, etc.)
- Building apps or major development you've done just for fun
- Coding side projects on GitHub or another sharing platform
- Building websites for nonprofits, schools, or local businesses

- Competing in strategy games (chess, etc.)
- Anything that highlights math, logic, or problem solving

Examples

The other activities section should only be two or three bullets. For an IT manager using this section to strengthen his general competencies, it might look like this:

OTHER ACTIVITES
- Coach middle school soccer team
- Volunteer as tour guide for Museum of Natural History

For a younger candidate who wants to show additional technical experience, it might look like this:

OTHER ACTIVITES
- Build side projects on GITHUB. Sample: github.com/author/sample-proj
- Participate in open source projects, including TensorFlow, a Google machine-learning software library

That's it. You don't want to make this section too long or it will look like you're either juggling too many things at once or deliberately trying to take up space due to a lack of work experience.

Turning an Activity into a Hook

A hiring manager I know recently admitted to me that he called a candidate in for an interview *based on a completely irrelevant item listed as an other activity on the resume*: The candidate had included "develop applications for iPhone and iPad" as an other activity. This particular candidate had built fully functional applications, posted them to the App Store, and regularly received incoming royalties. What a hook! Imagine how many IT professionals have thought about doing something like that themselves. Here is a candidate who knows the process and how to get started.

If you participate in any activities that could be considered hooks, be sure to list them. *Even if an activity is only loosely related to the job, you might hook the reader by generating personal interest.*

Controversial Topics

In general, do not include anything that could remotely be considered political or controversial. Yes, it is illegal for hiring managers to discriminate based on these things, but it is very difficult to prove. So to be safe, leave it off.

The one exception would be if you want to deliberately screen employers and rule out those who don't share your same ideals. For example, let's say you volunteered extensively at Planned Parenthood and are a deep believer in this organization's mission. You might include this on your resume, being fully aware that a more conservative hiring manager will be turned off by it. You'll be less likely to be hired, but maybe that's okay since you're only interested in companies who share your ideals.

Coming up with Material

What if you really don't do that much outside of work or school? If not, don't make things up. Instead, take action! Volunteering or getting involved is easier than you may think. If you need to add balance to your resume, then join a community activity. Or if you need to show more technical experience, then get involved with an open source project. Get the ball rolling now, and soon you'll be able to legitimately put it on your resume. Plus, you might actually have some fun along the way!

Chapter 11

Putting it all Together

H opefully you've been building your resume a little bit in each section, as we've gone along, or at least have been jotting down some notes. If not, then the time for action has finally arrived!

Writing a Rough Draft

Writer's block is common with resume writing, and the first word is absolutely the hardest. But once you get going, it should really take only an hour to knock out your entire rough draft. Your rough draft will be *rough*, and that is perfectly okay. Capturing your *ideas* is the important thing at this stage, not the grammar or flow. Don't worry if it doesn't sound quite right and don't worry about formatting yet. Just try to get everything onto paper that you can think of.

Find a time and a place where you will be uninterrupted for one hour. In fact, since you're sitting down to read this book, *right now* is probably a good time. So fire up your computer or even go old school, and get out a pen and paper. No more procrastinating. Take an hour right now and get that resume rolling!

Editing and Proofreading

Once you've completed your rough draft (and subsequent drafts), you'll need to edit and proofread. Some guidelines:

1) Use little words if they will do. Many writers use big words mistakenly believing they sound better. Remember, recruiters may read hundreds of resumes in a single day, and big words are exhausting to read. If you can accurately convey your thoughts using little words, then don't be afraid to do so.

2) Use one word if it will do. Many writers also mistakenly add redundant words into their resumes. Don't do this. For example, don't say "developed and programmed reports", or "led and managed projects".

3) But use two words if you need to. For example, you might say "designed and developed reports". This is perfectly okay because *designed* and *developed* are distinctly different concepts.

4) Use parallel structure in your writing. This means that you should use the same form in bullet points or in lists. For example, you might say "designed interfaces, wrote reports, and created supporting documentation". This is parallel because all three items in the list start with a verb and end with a noun. But if you omit the verb in one of the items in the list, it is no longer parallel. It would <u>not</u> be okay to say, "designed interfaces, reports, and created supporting documentation".

5) Be consistent with spelling and punctuation. For example, both "online" and "on-line" are correct, but whichever you use, you need to be consistent. If you follow your bullets with periods, then follow *all* of your bullets with periods.

One more thing -- always have someone else review your final product to catch anything that you might have missed! Beware of misused words that aren't caught by automated spell checkers. For example, I recently saw a resume with the job title, "Project Manger". I'm sure this candidate thought everything was fine, but that resume went straight into the circular file.

Getting to a Final Draft

Turning your rough draft into a final draft is a process that typically takes about a week. Each day, you'll think of something new, so update your resume at least once a day. During this time, read Part Three to learn how to tailor your resume to specific types of IT jobs that you might be interested in. Update your resume accordingly.

As you get closer to a final draft, you'll trim material down to one to two pages (or as discussed in Chapter 3, a little longer for consulting resumes). If by the end of your editing, you still can't fit to your desired page length, do not reduce the font size to anything below 11. Tiny fonts, like big words, are tiring to read. Keep trimming and editing. If necessary, it's better to spill over into another page than to use a tiny font size.

Keep your original material. Any extra bullet points that didn't make the final cut can be used in customized versions of your resume.

See Appendix D for a simple example of a completed resume.

Customizing your Resume for Each Job

Finally, customize your resume not only to the job type, but to each specific job you apply for. This is actually pretty easy. Just do this:

1) Review the job requisition. Print a copy and circle the job title, skills, and required duties that they call out.

2) Include the job title on your resume in such a way that it sounds like you are introducing yourself as that job title. Use a title that is close to, or exactly the same as, the title they use.

See Chapter 6 for more information on including a job title in your resume.

3) Add skills they mention to your skills list. Add as many as you can while still being truthful. Use the *exact* words they use.

4) Make minor tweaks to the other sections of your resume based on the required duties that they call out. Demonstrate that you have performed these duties successfully.

5) Save the customized resume in a separate folder. Choose the filename carefully, because if the resume is sent electronically, the filename will be the first thing the recruiter or hiring manager will see. Include your first and last name in the filename. Instead of the word "resume", include the target job title in the filename. As in step #2, you are conveying that you consider this to be your primary job title, which just happens to match the job requisition. For example, "Brittany Wright Project Manager" or "Jim Bennet Developer".

Chapter 12

Submitting Your Resume

O kay, so your resume is now complete and I bet it looks pretty amazing! The next step is to get it in front of some potential employers. There are five basic ways to do this:

1) Through a colleague
2) Through a connection
3) Through an IT agency
4) Directly through the company's website
5) By posting your resume to a job board

Submitting Your Resume Through a Colleague

If you have a friend or colleague who already works at your target company, then pass your resume along to that person via email, with a very short cover letter, or "cover note". Below is an example of a great cover note:

Hi Karen, I saw you guys just posted for a new developer. Would you mind passing along my resume to the hiring manager and putting in a good word for me? I'm super interested and would be forever grateful if you could help me out. Thank you! Jim.

Notice how informal it is. I bet it's the shortest cover letter you've ever seen! It works because *they know each other*. Jim doesn't need to sell himself. Jim and Karen have worked together in the past, and presumably Karen already knows Jim's capabilities. He lets her know that he is very interested and closes with a double dose of thanks. That's it.

Submitting your resume to a colleague is *by far* the best way to go. If you have a strong relationship, your colleague will forward your resume to the hiring manager with a sentence or two saying that she knows you and thinks you'll do a good job. This puts your resume at the top of the stack, right in the front of the hiring manager, with a personal referral. In other words, it's the absolute jackpot! Generally, you'll also have to send your resume through the formal HR formal process, but the hiring manager will now shepherd you through the hoops. Your odds of getting an interview will go up several times.

Unfortunately, when contacting colleagues, you'll also commonly get the "polite brush-off", especially with those whom you might not know that well. They'll say it was good to hear from you and then nicely point you to their website or HR department. This is not the desired response, but when it happens, all is not lost. Just submit your resume through the formal channel as requested, then respond back to them and ask once again to put in a good word for you. You might get the referral anyway.

What if you don't know whether you know anyone at your target company? In this case, LinkedIn can be an invaluable resource. When you find a job you're interested in, log in to your LinkedIn account and key in the company's name in the search box. **LinkedIn will pull back anyone from your network who works there.** Frequently, it will turn up people you didn't expect, for example, colleagues from several years ago who may have recently moved over to the company you are targeting.

Submitting Your Resume Through a Connection

LinkedIn will also show you 2nd degree connections (i.e. friends of friends). You can click on the "shared connections" icon to see who connects you. This is a great way to locate someone inside your target company who might be able to help you out.

For example, you might find Darren Smith as a 2nd degree connection at your target company. You don't know him directly, but you know Christine Jones, and LinkedIn says that Christine is your link to Darren. So all you need to do is see if Christine would be willing to introduce you to Darren! LinkedIn provides a way to make online introductions, but meeting in real life is even better. Suggest meeting for coffee. Let Darren know you're interested in working at his company, and see if he's willing to pass your resume along.

You might think this is asking a lot and maybe you're wondering why anyone would be willing to help you out. There are two reasons. First, many companies offer referral bonuses. If someone forwards on your resume and you get hired, that person might get $1000 or more as a bonus. Second, business savvy people recognize that by helping you find a job, they are indirectly helping themselves too. Someday they might need a job and you might be in a position to return the favor.

Submitting Your Resume Through an IT Agency

Another good option is to submit your resume through an IT agency, or staffing firm. These firms are matchmakers between candidates and employers. They employ their own recruiters to find potential candidates on behalf of numerous employers (who are their clients).

Good IT agencies maintain relationships not only with their clients' HR departments, but also directly with IT hiring managers. If they've had a successful track record filling previous positions, then *their opinions will matter* -- they'll have wide-open doors to the people who ultimately make hiring decisions. When a trusted agency passes along your resume with a good word, it's almost like a personal referral. You'll likely get that interview.

The trick to utilizing IT agency recruiters is to build relationships with recruiters *while you are employed.* When recruiters contact you, you might feel like it's a nuisance, but it only takes a minute to respond. Link to them on LinkedIn and thank them for considering you as a candidate. Politely let them know you're currently employed, and you'll keep their information should your situation change. If they want to meet for coffee or lunch, go ahead and meet them. Recruiters have the pulse of the IT market, and maintaining solid relationships with a couple recruiters can be invaluable.

Submitting Your Resume Directly

If you can't find someone on the inside, then you are left with the option of submitting your resume directly. This generally means filling out an online job application and uploading your resume to the company's website.

Under this option, you're basically thrown in with the masses. Your resume will be entered into a database with possibly dozens of other resumes for the same open job requisition. Even if your resume is amazing (which it should be!), you're still basically rolling the dice here. They might have twenty resumes that all match on the key search words, so it is quite possible that *your resume won't be viewed at all.* If it is viewed, it will really need to stand out for you to get selected for an interview.

Use this option sparingly. Whenever possible, it is much better to get a colleague, connection, or IT agency to personally pass your resume along to a hiring manager.

Posting Your Resume to a Job Board

There is one final option. In addition to responding to specific job requisitions, you can also post your resume "out there" for any potential employer to see. Proponents of this method say this vastly increases your exposure, giving you instant access to hundreds of available jobs.

This might sound great, but posting your resume to a job board exposes your resume to all kinds of people that you don't personally know or trust. Recruiters like to present good resumes because doing so shows that they have personal connections to good people. But unscrupulous recruiters are out there too, and they might present your resume to clients without your permission. Worse, they might keep your resume in their own database and continue to present it over and over as a bait-and-switch resume. Other job-seekers can be pretty unethical, too, and may "hijack" your resume, cutting and pasting your qualifications into their own resume.

Philosophically, this is kind of a bad approach to finding a job anyway. A job is something you'll do for eight hours or more a day, for *years*. You should be *very* selective about finding a job. Identify companies you're interested in and go after them. Take a sniper approach, not a shotgun approach. Don't just post on a board and say "hey, I'm available -- does anyone want to hire me?" You'll just end up getting a ton of spam. If you want your dream job, you have to put in effort and go find it!

A Note about Professional Networking

You may have noticed that the more successful methods of submitting your resume *require you to know someone*. Like it or not, most IT jobs are still filled by "who you know". So networking and maintaining a professional presence on LinkedIn are absolute requirements these days. Networking and LinkedIn are mostly beyond the scope of this book, but there are many other great books out there on these topics.

Part Three

Resumes for Specific IT Jobs

Chapter 13

Jobs in Information Technology

I n Part Three, we'll discuss how to tailor your resume to the type of IT job you're applying for.

If you're new to IT, you might be wondering what kinds of IT jobs are out there in the first place. Maybe you know a couple of administrators or software engineers, but don't really understand exactly what they do. Or you might already work in IT, but you're in one small corner of a giant IT department, and wonder how your work fits in with what everyone else is doing. If you're a little confused about this, you're not alone -- Many IT veterans, even some *CIOs*, don't know who does what!

So let's take a minute to clear this up.

We'll use an analogy. Imagine you run a construction company and are developing a new home community. Before anyone picks up a hammer and nails, several steps must happen. First, you'll have someone *analyze* the landscape. This person will look into construction trends, meet with consumers, and figure out what needs to be built. Next, one of your employees will *design* the house. This person will write up blueprints illustrating the layout of the rooms and the necessary building materials. Then the builders will *build*. These people will put up the walls and install electric and plumbing. Finally, once the customer moves in, you'll make someone available to provide *support*. This person will answer questions, handle warranty issues, and take care of follow-up items.

So home construction takes four main steps – analyze, design, build, and support. Developing IT systems takes the same four steps:

- **Analyze**. The **business analyst** figures out what needs to be built. She meets with users, understands requirements, and determines the business problem that needs to be solved. *Systems analyst* is another term for business analyst.

- **Design**. The **technical analyst** designs what is going to be built. He writes up specs outlining screen flow, programming logic, and supporting reports. *Web designer, user experience designer, user interface designer,* and *systems designer* are all various specialties within this role. A role that combines both analysis and design is typically called a *business/technical analyst* or *software engineer*.

- **Build**. The **developer** builds the working product. He writes code to render the screens, perform calculations, and pull data from databases. *Programmer* is a term that is loosely synonymous, although that job title usually implies slightly less scope in decision-making. A *programmer analyst* is someone who performs both design and development.

- **Support**. The **support specialist** provides user support for the product. He or she answers questions, handles requests for help, and resolves customer issues. *Helpdesk analyst* and *helpdesk technician* are other names for a support specialist.

In addition to building, the IT department needs additional hands simply to "keep the lights on". These people work in Infrastructure and Management:

- **Infrastructure**. Think about all of the things that must run smoothly every day in an IT department. Administrators monitor these things and keep them operating efficiently. A *systems administrator* handles servers; a *network administrator* handles networks; and a *database administrator* handles the database. The terms *architect* and *engineer* are similar but imply a greater level of responsibility and more experience. For example, a *network engineer* not only maintains existing networks but would also design new networks.

- **Management**. Managers, of course, manage. A *project manager* is responsible for a specific project, and a *program manager* oversees multiple projects. Each sub-department within IT also typically has a manager. Common examples are *Manager of Support, Manager of Applications*, and *Manager of Ecommerce*. Groups of managers are overseen by *IT directors*, and at larger organizations, groups of IT directors are overseen by *vice presidents*.

So we have analyze, design, build, support, infrastructure, and management. These six job categories can be grouped together into the following diagram:

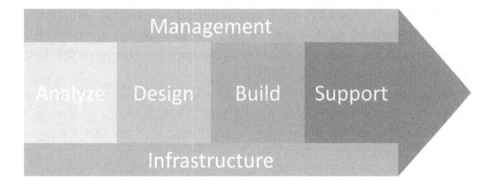

Almost everyone in any IT department, big or small, will work in one of these six areas. Some IT jobs, such as a support specialist, fall clearly into one box. Others fall on the border between multiple boxes. For example, a programmer analyst, as discussed above, does both design and development, so would fit halfway between Design and Build.

Here are the more common IT jobs and how they fit into the diagram:

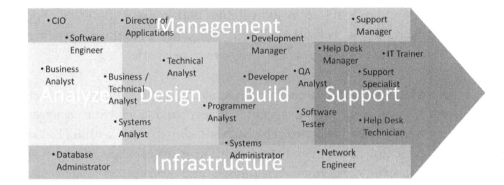

Using Part Three of this Book

In each of the next chapters, we'll dive into a specific box from the above diagram (analyze and design are covered together in a single chapter). We'll discuss what competencies recruiters and hiring managers look for in that type of job, and how to tailor your career summary, skills, and professional experience to give you the best chance at landing that type of job.

Since there is a lot of overlap among IT job responsibilities, it's a good idea to read Part Three all the way through, but if you're in a hurry, feel free to flip to the specific section or sections that are most relevant to you.

Chapter 14

Resumes for Business / Technical Analysts

I f you're looking for a job as a business analyst, technical analyst, systems analyst, systems designer, or software engineer, then this section is for you. A business analyst typically works with business users to understand requirements, then determines the high-level direction for the IT solution. A technical analyst converts those requirements to detailed technical specifications. If the company has an ERP system, such as SAP, then the technical analyst will also configure the system.

The distinction is blurring between a business and a technical analyst, so we will handle them together here in one chapter. In either case, you should give plenty of attention to both your business and technical competencies. Even if you are a "pure" technical analyst, you'll still need you to work directly with business users from time to time. Plus, hiring managers are always looking to save on budget, and if you can show that you're strong on both sides, then the hiring manager may be able to consolidate positions, saving money.

A business/technical analyst requires one of the most well-rounded competency profiles. In addition to your business and technical competencies, you must be a self-starter. To a large degree, you need to figure out what to work on, often with very little direction from a manager. You must get along well with both IT and business people, and will need to manage by persuasion, achieving results with people who aren't your direct subordinates. Your target competency profile looks like this:

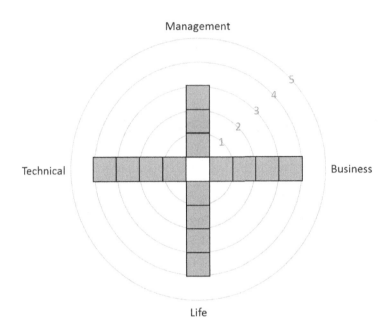

On your resume, be sure to highlight:

- Industry knowledge. This is one of the few positions where industry knowledge is at least as important as technical know-how. If you're going to improve how the business operates, you need to understand how it operates in the first place! Mention the industries associated with your previous positions, along with your company's position within them. If you've worked for manufacturing or distribution companies, demonstrate that you understand their manufacturing and distribution strategies. If you've worked for retail, call out something about this industry, such as pricing or assortment planning. Your resume should clearly convey that you know best practices across a number of industries.

- Technical skills. As a business/technical analyst, you must also act as the bridge between business understanding and technical solutions. You need to be able to design databases, screens, reports, interfaces, and applications. If the company has an ERP system, you'll need to configure that as well. Show that you have this expertise. Call out specific systems you have designed in enough detail to convey complexities involved. In addition, be sure to indicate which software packages and modules you have configured.

- Ability to work without supervision. At many companies, business/technical analysts receive almost no direction at all. It is *your job* to proactively seek out the business and look for ways to improve it. Show a potential employer that you can take a vaguely identified need, formulate it into a project, get the project underway, and ultimately deliver it successfully. Mention that you reach out to users and company leaders to gather requirements. Show that you are the kind of employee who builds your own list of what to work on, rather than waiting for it to come to you.

- Business improvement track record. This is a key differentiator between a novice analyst and an experienced one. A novice analyst simply replaces old systems with something newer. But an experienced analyst delivers solutions *that result in sustained business improvement.* Have you been part of projects that have increased sales, reduced inventories, shortened fulfillment times, or improved customer satisfaction? Can you quantify results that were achieved? If so, these will be very strong selling points on your resume.

Career Summary

To convey these ideas, a career summary for a business/technical analyst might look something like this:

> Proven leader with 12 year track record of delivering sustained business improvement. Supply chain and manufacturing experience combined with technical know-how required to implement IT solutions. Think creatively, take initiative, and work with minimal direction.

Or maybe like this:

> Experienced consultant with rare combination of industry best practices and IT expertise. Ten years of experience with improvement methodologies such as Six Sigma, Lean, and Business Process Reengineering. Self-starter who takes initiative, thinks outside the box, and delivers results.

See Appendix A for additional career summary phrases.

Skills

The skills section for a business/technical analyst should be well balanced. Start with business skills, then follow with two or three rows of general technical skills. Round out the list with a couple of management skills. Unlike resumes for many other IT jobs, your skills section should have very little techno-jargon. Your completed skills section might look like this:

- Business process design
- Manufacturing strategies
- Six Sigma
- Transportation planning
- Integration testing
- Data conversion
- Team management
- Business process Improvement
- Retail assortment planning
- Supply chain optimization
- Sales order processing
- Business Intelligence
- Master data management
- Business metrics

See Appendix B for a list of additional skills.

Professional Experience

As discussed in Chapter 8, you will start each job on your resume with a role overview. For a business/technical analyst, you should always mention the industry, which shows business competency. For example:

> Led both IT and business improvement initiatives for this leading chemical manufacturer. Optimized manufacturing, distribution, and procurement processes.

For each job, bullet out accomplishments that uniquely reflect your own experience. Once you have jotted down basic bullet points, expand each one and turn it into a *hook,* as described in Chapter 8. Show that you have solved a common business problem. *Articulate the business result.* Where possible, add in metrics and numbers.

Examples of starting bullet points:
- Participated in inventory reduction project
- Built error-checks into sales order entry
- Implemented new business unit on SAP
- Designed new reports

Examples of expanded bullet points:
- Implemented inventory postponement strategy. Lowered inventory by 30% while maintaining service level.

- Built automated checks into sales order process to trap frequently occurring errors. Reduced sales order entry time by 50% and error rate by 70%.

- Implemented SAP for European business unit. Rollout included 3 customer services centers and 14 warehouses in 6 countries.

- Designed suite of master data reports to guarantee consistency across customers, vendors and materials.

These examples contain multiple hooks. Notice the problems being solved – inventory levels, sales order entry errors, multinational complexity, master data consistency. These are common enough problems that a hiring manager is likely to be hooked by at least one of them. See Chapter 8 for more information on turning your bullets into hooks.

Most of your bullet points should focus on projects and accomplishments, but you'll also want to add two or three task bullet points throughout your resume. Task bullet points highlight your technical competency and provide an excuse to list buzzwords that may get picked up on resume screening software. Examples:

- Designed reports, interfaces, enhancements, and data conversion programs.

- Configured SD, and MM modules within SAP. Focused on sales order entry, pricing, shipping, procurement, and inventory management.

- Handled integration between PROS and JDA (Red Prairie) systems.

Finally, to round out your Professional Experience section, think about things you may have done that demonstrate leadership, initiative, or interpersonal skills. Sprinkle in a couple of bullet points to call some attention to your life competency. Examples:

- Presented options and recommendations to executive leadership team.

- Delivered training to 40 sales representatives.

- Traveled throughout rollout and acted as support liaison for 5 separate sites.

Chapter 15

Resumes for Developers

I f you're looking for a job as a developer or programmer, then this section is for you. Developers use a number of languages and tools to build applications. In some cases, you may be applying for a job at a company that uses exactly what you've used before; in others, the tools or languages will be different. But in almost all cases, at least some of your technical expertise will be transferrable into the new job.

The first thing you will highlight, of course, are your technical skills. Call out specific languages, software packages, tools, and platforms, since these will be picked up when your resume is screened by computers. Communicate that you are able to code complicated logic efficiently and that you understand how your programs connect to other modules, systems, or databases.

But you don't want to sound like a techno-robot. Your competency profile leans technical but isn't *all* technical. You must show that you have enough general business knowledge to understand the purpose of your programs and how they fit into the big picture. In addition, you'll need to demonstrate thoroughness and accountability, attributes in the life competency. Your target competency profile looks like this:

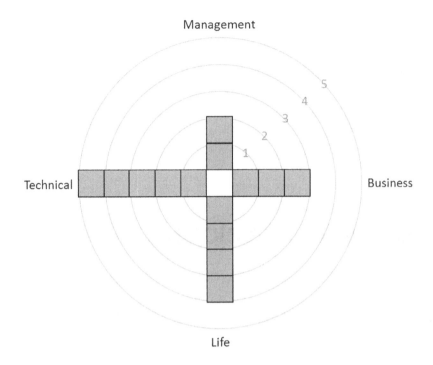

On your resume, be sure to highlight:

- Business acumen. Show the hiring manager that you are the kind of developer that can work directly with business users. You not only code from specs, but you also create your own designs. You appreciate how the business users will interact with your program, and you understand the business benefits that your program will deliver. Demonstrate that you aren't just a programming machine – You can plug design gaps, make suggestions, and improve programs.

- Quality of work and accountability. IT departments lose millions of dollars and countless hours to rework. Show that you are the kind of developer who reads the spec carefully, clarifies areas of confusion before starting development, and unit tests thoroughly. Also, be sure to convey that you have a sense of urgency and accountability. Demonstrate that you deliver your work on time and resolve issues quickly.

- Interpersonal skills. Show that you have the ability to get along with your team, and also *to get along with your manager.* A hiring manager I know periodically drops by her employees' desks to see what they're working on. Frequently, she receives this answer: "It's really technical, you wouldn't understand." As you might imagine, she doesn't like this answer at all! Make sure your resume doesn't come across with this kind of arrogance. Convey that you are someone who is excited about your work and would gladly take a few minutes to share with your manager.

- Balance. Developers have a reputation for extremes. Some are sloppy. Their code is disorganized, their testing shoddy, and their documentation nonexistent. Others are perfectionists. Although they deliver quality work, they are difficult to work with, getting easily frustrated and missing deadlines. You may know some developers at one extreme or the other. Hopefully you're somewhere in the middle. Communicate that you take a pragmatic and balanced approach. Your work is thorough, but you are also aware of deadlines and priorities. You live in the real world and are willing to make tradeoffs when necessary.

Career Summary

To convey these ideas, a career summary for a developer might look something like this:

Senior developer with 10 years of experience building software to solve business problems. Detailed, thorough, and able to meet deadlines in demanding and fast paced environments. Quick learner with excellent communication skills.

Or maybe like this:

> Respected developer with 10 years of IT success. Deep expertise in multiple programming languages combined with real-world business know-how. Strong sense of accountability and drive to meet deadlines. Energetic team player who works hard but also has fun on the job.

See Appendix A for additional career summary phrases.

Skills

The skills section for a developer should be technical, but not overly so. Start with general technical skills that almost any IT professional would understand. Then follow with your core bullets, outlining specific languages. This is where you hit them with the techno-jargon. Round it out with a couple of management or business skills. Your skills list might look something like this:

- GUI design
- XML
- IOS / Swift
- CSS
- Creative thinking

- Database design
- C++, C#
- SQL, MySQL
- Visual Studio
- Leadership

- Mobile development
- HTML, DHTML
- Java, JavaScript
- Business metrics
- Self-motivation

See Appendix B for a list of additional skills.

Professional Experience

As discussed in Chapter 8, you will start each job with a role overview. In the role overview, touch on both the business and technical aspects of your position. For example:

> Developed shop floor execution functionality for leading automotive supplies company. Support manufacturing line that produces over 5000 units per day and supplies parts to almost every major automobile manufacturer.

For each job, bullet out accomplishments that uniquely reflect your own experience. Once you have jotted down basic bullet points, expand each one and turn it into a *hook,* as described in Chapter 8. Show that you understand the larger context of your work. Discuss the business problem that you are solving and explain what makes it complex. *Articulate the business result.* Where possible, add in metrics and numbers.

Examples of starting bullet points:
- Built interface to MES system
- Designed report to merge MES and Oracle data
- Coded sales comp and commission enhancement
- Built forecasting tool

Examples of expanded bullet points:
- Built interface to manufacturing execution system (MES) to collect real-time temperature and meter readings from shop floor machines.

- Designed custom report that merged MES and Oracle data to determine recurring causes of production defects. Helped reduce defects by 9% in the first year.

- Built enhancement to handle sales compensation and commissions. Supported variable commissions, draws, and other complex arrangements.

- Designed forecasting cockpit used by CFO to provide estimated results to shareholders.

These examples contain multiple hooks. Notice the problems being solved – capturing production data, reducing defects, sales compensation, commissions, forecasting, and estimating period-end results. These are common enough problems that a typical hiring manager is likely to be hooked by at least one of them. See Chapter 8 for more information on turning your bullets into hooks.

Most of your bullet points should focus on projects and accomplishments, but you'll also want to add in task bullets at the bottom of each job. Task bullet points highlight your technical competency and give you an excuse to list buzzwords that may get picked up on resume screening software. Examples:

- Built numerous additional programs using C++ and Java.

- Frequently worked with incomplete designs and plugged gaps as necessary.

- Executed unit tests, documented results, and resolved issues.

- Conducted peer-reviews on team members' code.

Finally, to round out your Professional Experience section, think about things you may have done that demonstrate leadership, initiative, or interpersonal skills. Sprinkle in a couple of bullet points to call attention to your life competency. Examples:

- Co-developed code review and naming standards.

- Created onboarding process for new team members.

- Prepared user training manual that outlined the company history, business processes, and software features.

- Participated in company mentorship program. Mentored 5 new developers in 3 years.

Chapter 16

Resumes for Support Specialists

I f you're looking for a job as a support specialist, helpdesk technician, or helpdesk analyst, this section is for you. In smaller organizations, a single support specialist may handle just about everything – installations, hardware issues, software issues, network problems, and general IT questions. In larger organizations, support specialists are typically arranged into tiers by depth of expertise.

A tier 1 support specialist answers incoming calls at the help desk. He or she gathers customer information, records symptoms, and solves basic problems such as password resets. More complex problems get routed to tier 2 analysts, who have more experience and are more specialized. The most complex problems get routed to tier 3. Tier 3 analysts generally have a lot of leeway in determining how to solve problems. They may work with developers, or call on consultants, vendors, or colleagues for assistance.

The support specialist is the only true customer service position within IT. It requires patience, good communication skills, and the ability to stay calm under pressure. For a support specialist, the life competency is even more important than technical. Your target competency profile looks like this:

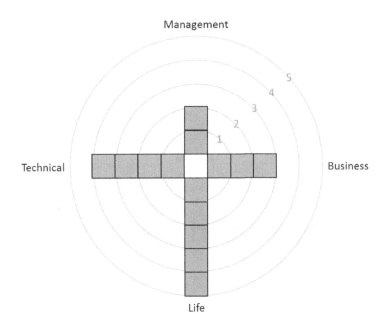

On your resume, be sure to highlight:

- Customer service background. Things get hectic at the support desk. An issue may spread like wildfire, and some days, the phones will ring off the hook with dozens, or even hundreds of people experiencing the same issue. But this doesn't bother you — *you stay cool under pressure*. Show that you can handle the stress of working on the help desk, and that even when things are crazy, you deliver a consistent customer service experience. At many companies, users rate support specialists on helpfulness, expertise, and overall satisfaction. If you've worked at a prior help desk and have received good scores on these kinds of metrics, be sure to call attention to them.

- Ability to work without supervision. Things also get boring at the help desk. You may go several hours without a single new issue, and you may see whole weeks where almost nothing goes wrong. Show that during these quiet times, you don't just sit around and wait — you take initiative and get things done. You practice *proactive support*. During quiet times, you reach out to customers and look for ways to enhance the overall customer service experience. You continually build your technical skills, hone your soft skills, and improve how the department operates.

- Analysis skills. This is a key differentiator between a novice support specialist and an expert one. A novice support specialist pushes through the issues one by one. But an expert support specialist looks for links among the issues, attempts to tie them back to a root cause, then *finds a solution for the root cause*. An expert support specialist may kill two, three, or twenty birds with one stone. Demonstrate that you have the analysis skills to do just that. Call out a specific issue that you might have solved. Use enough detail to convey what was solved, why it was complex, and how you figured it out.

- Ability to learn quickly. You never know what you're going to get on the help desk. Maybe you've done hardware installations your whole career, and now you're assigned to a new help desk handling software upgrades. Or maybe the new help desk supports totally different hardware *and* software than what you are used to. Many times, being able to come up to speed quickly is even more important than your existing technical skill base. Highlight your ability to learn quickly and your passion for learning. Show that you are flexible, adaptable, and always willing to take on a new challenge.

Career Summary

To convey these ideas, a career summary for a support specialist might look something like this:

Exceptional support specialist with eight years of experience. Have worked all facets of support including tiers 1, 2, and 3, hardware, software, and infrastructure. Proactively implement solutions to resolve problems before they are raised as issues. Quick learner who takes initiative and stays calm under pressure.

Or maybe like this:

Multi-certified support professional who attacks problems, determines root causes, and implements corrective measures. Proven track record delivering an exceptional customer service experience in hardware, software, and network support. Perform thorough analysis, learn quickly, and stay calm under pressure.

Skills

The skills section for a support specialist should open with life and business skills such as *customer service* and *complaint handling*. Then follow with your technical proficiencies—network technologies, operating systems, desktop applications, browsers, and incident management systems that you know how to support. Your completed skills section might look like this:

- Customer service
- User training
- LAN and WI-FI
- MS Edge, Safari
- Windows, Unix, Citrix

- Active listening
- OS installation
- Hardware configuration
- PCs, Laptops
- Remedy, Freshdesk

- Complaint handling
- Databases (Oracle,SQL)
- Remote connectivity
- Telephony systems
- Production support

Due to the nature of the job, support specialists may want to highlight many more skills compared to other IT professionals. You may have supported a vast number of different technologies, more than would reasonably fit in two columns. If so, then group your skills into categories, as shown below:

General Skills:	Customer service, user training, support, complaints handling, troubleshooting, technical diagnosis.
Operating systems:	Windows, Unix, iOS
Software:	MS Office, Google Docs, SAP, Oracle, Salesforce
Browsers:	Safari, Firefox, Chrome, MS Edge

Networking: VPN, LAN, WAN, Wi-Fi, Citrix, Remote connectivity

Incident Resolution: JIRA, HEAT, Remedy, Freshdesk

See Appendix B for a list of additional skills.

Professional Experience

As discussed in Chapter 8, you will start each job with a role overview. Include numbers of users, sites, or geographies supported to give the reader an idea of the scope of your role. For example:

> Handled a wide range of hardware, software, and connectivity issues for this nationwide retailer. Supported over 1000 users at 70 sites 24x7.

For each job, bullet accomplishments that uniquely reflect your own experience. Once you have jotted down basic bullet points, expand each one and turn it into a *hook,* as described in Chapter 8. Be sure to call out complexities involved, and also the *result* of your work, such as reduced downtime or increased efficiency. If you previously worked at another help desk, call out your service metrics.

Examples of starting bullet points:
- Handled incoming service calls
- Resolved hardware problems
- Deployed PCs and other hardware

Examples of expanded bullet points:
- Handled incoming service calls. Received "Excellent" rating in customer satisfaction and achieved first-call resolution rate of 70%.

- Initiated preventive maintenance schedule to address ongoing hardware problems. Reduced user downtime by 20%.

- Deployed PCs, Zebra label printers, handheld devices, barcode readers, and other hardware.

These examples contain multiple hooks. We see strong customer service metrics and a candidate who is proactive – he knows the importance of preventive maintenance versus just fighting fires. The bottom bullet calls out label printers, handheld devices, and barcode readers, all *targeted hooks* aimed at hiring managers who are responsible for supporting these types of technology. See Chapter 8 for more information on turning your bullets into hooks.

In addition to their day-to-day work, support specialists also often participate in projects. Be sure to mention any projects that you've been a part of, which will demonstrate a larger scope of responsibility. Examples:

- Upgraded 250 PCs from Windows 8 to Windows 10.

- Participated in hardware refresh. Deployed new laptops to over 1000 users.

- Installed 60 phones and configured VoIP for new corporate office.

Finally, to round out your Professional Experience section, think about things you may have done that demonstrate leadership, initiative, or interpersonal skills. Sprinkle in a couple of bullet points to call attention to your life competency. Examples:

- Provided bulletins, classroom training, and online support to educate users about recurring issues.

- Transitioned to new incident management software. One of two support specialists assigned to implementation team.

- Attended two weeks of customer service training. Topics included building customer loyalty, complaint handling, effective communication, and proactive resolution.

Chapter 17

Resumes for Infrastructure Jobs

I f you're looking for a job in infrastructure, then this section is for you. Infrastructure jobs are the ones that keep things up and running in IT departments. They include network administrators, database administrators, and systems administrators, along with architects and engineers across those same categories. At a small company, a single person may handle all infrastructure needs. At a larger company, dozens, or even hundreds of people might be employed in this area.

These are the most technical of the technical jobs. Infrastructure jobs are what most people imagine when you tell them you work in IT — the guy who monitors rooms full of giant computers with blinking lights and whirring tape drives.

Working in infrastructure requires a lot more than just technical expertise, however. Getting the job done generally requires multiple people, so you must be able to manage, or at least influence others to achieve necessary results. You must be proactive and make use of calm times to maintain, upgrade, and improve. As you move up the ladder, you'll focus as much on budget control as you do on technology. Your competency profile will lean technical, but you must also highlight the other competencies. Your target competency profile looks like this:

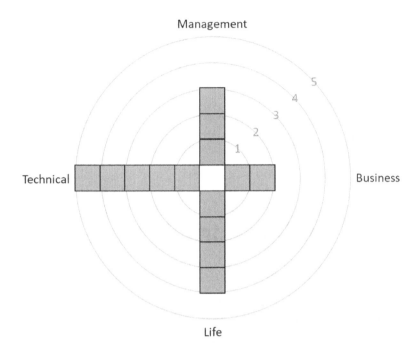

On your resume, be sure to highlight:

- Proactivity. In many infrastructure jobs, if you're doing your job well, there are no emergencies. Whatever it is that you support — databases, servers, networks — are all running smoothly. You can take a day off without everything falling to pieces. But rather than sit on your heels, this is the time when you really shine! Demonstrate that you use downtime to proactively look for bottlenecks and come up with solutions, making the overall landscape even better. You patch, upgrade, and repair your systems. Show that you put in hard work day in and day out, which is *why* you don't have as many emergencies.

- Focus on the cost side of the equation. Bandwidth, performance, speed, redundancy, and uptime aren't free. Most companies don't need the best systems and networks in the world. What they want is *good systems and networks at a reasonable cost*. So be sure to call attention to your relentless focus on keeping costs in check. Discuss initiatives you've launched or procedures you've implemented that have cut costs. Highlight any vendor negotiation you've been a part of, especially if you negotiated contracts that saved your employer money.

- Critical thinking. Infrastructure jobs require a logical, methodical approach to solving problems. When documents get stuck in the print queue, for example, a novice administrator clears out the print queue. But an experienced administrator *figures out why it is happening and implements a change that will keep it from happening again in the future.* Demonstrate that you don't just fix the problem, you address the *root cause.* Have you implemented long-term fixes to these kinds of problems? If so, be sure to call out enough detail to convey what the problems were, how you solved them, and why they required critical thinking.

- Interpersonal skills. Like developers, infrastructure administers have a reputation for being too technical. Yes, you need to know the techie nuts and bolts, but you also need to understand and work with your customers. Show that you regularly interact with a variety of non-technical people, including business users, department managers, and company leaders. Include some non-technical tasks. In addition, be sure to specifically call out the phrase *communication skills* or *interpersonal skills* somewhere in your resume.

Career Summary

To convey all of these ideas, a career summary for an infrastructure job might look something like this:

Certified Network Architect who delivers superior network availability and performance at a reasonable cost. Proactive troubleshooter who analyzes potential bottlenecks and implements solutions before problems appear. Hard-worker with excellent communication skills and passion for life-long learning.

Or maybe like this:

Respected Systems Administrator with 20 years of IT success. Real-world thinker who delivers solid system performance while keeping costs in check. Energetic worker, positive attitude, and excellent interpersonal skills.

See Appendix A for additional career summary phrases.

Skills

The skills you list will depend on whether your focus area is database, network, systems, or a combination of the three. Start with general technical skills that almost any IT professional would understand. Then follow with techno-jargon. At the bottom, include some management or life skills to round out your list. For a network administrator, for example, your skills list might look like this:

- Software installation
- Wi-Fi connectivity
- Database design
- Unix, Linux
- Vendor management
- Technical support
- IT authorizations
- Firewall administration
- Oracle, MySQL
- Problem diagnosis
- Troubleshooting
- Remote connectivity
- Network security
- Teambuilding
- Contract negotiation

See Appendix B for additional skills.

Professional Experience

As discussed in Chapter 8, you will start each job on your resume with a role overview. Include numbers of users, sites, or geographies supported to give the reader an idea of the scope of your role. For example:

Configured, maintained, and monitored hardware and systems for multi-site corporation with over 1000 users. Handled user accounts, upgrades, backups, and disaster recovery.

For each job, bullet out accomplishments that uniquely reflect your experience. Once you have jotted down basic bullet points, expand each one and turn it into a *hook,* as described in Chapter 8. Now for each bullet, articulate why the project mattered. Use non-technical (or at least semi-non-technical) language.

Examples of starting bullet points:
- Rolled out Wi-Fi signal boosters company-wide
- Established hybrid data center
- Implemented nightly database maintenance
- Negotiated new telecom contract
- Replaced in-house servers

Examples of expanded bullet points:
- Rolled out new Wi-Fi across entire retail chain. Doubled connection speed and almost completely eliminated dropped connections.

- Established hybrid data center. Hosted basic applications in the cloud, achieving 99.9% uptime, allowing the company to scale to peak-usage at lower cost.

- Implemented nightly automated maintenance. Improved database query speeds by over 100% with no expenditure.

- Negotiated new telecom contract, achieving the same level of service at 15% lower rate.

- Replaced in-house servers, increasing response time across the enterprise. Average time savings of 15 minutes per employee per day.

These examples contain some great hooks. In just a few bullet points, we touch on just about everything infrastructure hiring managers care about. This candidate is improving technical metrics while saving costs and helping the company to scale to meet growth. Bonus points for solving problems the hiring manager personally experiences, such as getting kicked off Wi-Fi.

Most of your bullet points should focus on projects and accomplishments, but you'll also want to add in task bullets to highlight your technical competency and work in some buzzwords that may get picked up on resume screening software. Examples:

- Install Unix upgrades and patches.
- Monitor network traffic, analyze bottlenecks, and conduct performance tuning.
- Set up user roles, authorizations, and security.

Now to round out your Professional Experience section, think about things you may have done that demonstrate leadership, initiative, or interpersonal skills. Sprinkle in a couple of bullet points to call attention to your life competency. Examples:

- Volunteered to write company procedure manuals. Created manuals for software installation, data recovery, and nightly jobs.
- Trained employees on VPN use, log-on procedures, and printer set-up.
- Presented data center options and recommendation to CIO. Performed thorough analysis on requirements, costs, and benefits.

Chapter 18

Resumes for IT Managers

I f you're looking for a job in IT management, then this is the section for you. IT management jobs include department managers, project managers, and program managers. Department managers oversee sub-departments within IT, making sure they provide the most value at a reasonable cost. Project managers ensure their projects stay on track and within budget. Program managers oversee multiple projects.

IT management requires an *entirely different set of skills* than IT hands-on work. So, if you are applying for a management position, **do not make the mistake of overselling your technical ability.** Even if you are superb technically, you don't want your resume to come across as too techie. Demonstrate your ability to achieve results not by doing the technical work yourself, but by *working through other people*.

Whether you're looking for a job managing support, applications, development, or any other area, your target competency profile is basically the same—well rounded with the most focus on management and the least on technical. Your target competency profile looks like this:

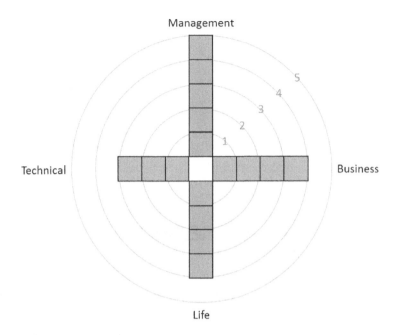

On your resume, be sure to highlight:

- Ability to prioritize. IT managers get inundated with requests. Novice managers are perpetually in a sink-or-swim state, sitting on a list ten times longer than they will ever be able to implement. They plough through the items one by one, hoping to someday get through them all. Great IT managers work differently. They combine request into projects, calculate ROI for each project, then ruthlessly prioritize. They understand that they may have to say no to a few important projects to clear room for the *most* important projects. Demonstrate that you prioritize this way. Call attention to any formal project approval processes that you may have implemented. Highlight your use of ROI calculations. Mention specific projects that you approved based on expected return.

- Implementation track record. A great manager works *on* the process, not in the process. If you're a development manager, for example, you don't just sit back and manage a bunch of developers. You initiate change, you make things better. In previous positions, did you implement a new methodology or training program? Did you put new metrics in place to better monitor your team's performance? Call attention to these types of things which show that you, as the manager, made your team more effective.

- Benefits realization. Most IT managers are finally understanding that IT projects should deliver tangible business benefit, such as increasing sales, reducing costs, or improving efficiency. However, once a project is complete, most IT managers still just move onto the next big thing. Only the best managers *follow up after is project is complete and confirm that benefits were actually realized*. Show that you perform this kind of follow up. Demonstrate that you monitor the post-go-live state, determine associated metrics, and *quantify* business results.

- Customer focus. Great IT managers spend up to half of their time with customers. Convey that you understand who your customers are and that you continually strengthen your relationships with them. Call attention to user groups you may have formed to provide input, or partnerships you've built with business leaders to jointly deliver projects. Show that customer feedback is an integral part of your operating procedure.

- Leadership. You might be able to prioritize well, initiate change, realize results, and do all this while keeping your customers in mind. But if your team hates working for you, then you'll never be a successful IT manager! The days are gone where you can drive your people into the ground to achieve results. Show that you are the kind of leader who people *enjoy* working for. Discuss teambuilding, mentoring, and putting a positive culture in place. Call attention to programs you may have established to ensure your team members are building new skills and growing in their careers.

Career Summary

To convey all of these ideas, a career summary for an IT manager might look something like this:

> Proven leader with a 10 year track record of implementation success. Initiate change, rapidly deliver IT solutions, and measure results. Excellent communicator who builds a climate of trust and brings out the best in teams.

Or maybe like this:

> Respected professional with 10 years of IT and business experience. Successfully build relationships with business leaders, lead large-scale projects, and deliver sustained business improvement. Energetic, adaptable leader who inspires team members to reach their potential.

See Appendix A for additional career summary phrases.

Skills

The skills section for an IT manager should primarily have managerial and business skills, with little or no techie acronyms. Include big-picture thinking skills such as *IT strategy* and *alignment of business and IT*, along with methodologies you may have used, such as *Agile*. Add a couple of skills that call attention to people-management or teambuilding. Round out your skills at the bottom with business-oriented skills. Your skills list might look something like this:

- Project/program management
- Business case development
- Teambuilding and mentoring
- Alignment of business and IT
- Agile methodology
- Supply chain execution
- Offshore management
- IT strategy
- Profit center management
- ROI analysis
- Business transformation
- Sales and distribution

See Appendix B for additional skills.

Professional Experience

As discussed in Chapter 8, you will start each job on your resume with a role overview. In the role overview, indicate your general scope of responsibility and call out numbers such as how many people were on your team or how many users you supported. For example:

> Led team of 9 developers who built and supported applications for 200 users. Responsible for ecommerce systems, Oracle/NetSuite modules, and custom applications.

Beneath your role overview, bullet accomplishments that uniquely reflect your experience. As a manager, you typically won't have many hands-on bullet points, so use phrases such as *carried out, sponsored, completed, directed,* or *oversaw* to indicate your role in the success of a project. See Appendix C for more management impact verbs. Once you have jotted down basic bullet points, expand each one and turn it into a *hook,* as described in Chapter 8. Articulate the business result and describe the impact, in terms of numbers.

Examples of starting bullet points:
- Prepared business cases for new projects
- Responsible for Oracle/NetSuite implementation
- Led EDI implementation
- Ran document management project
- Oversaw new website development

Examples of expanded bullet points:
- Established formal project approval process. Prepared business cases, quantified ROI, and selected only top-priority projects.

- Responsible for Oracle/NetSuite implementation. Delivered on time and within budget.

- Led EDI implementation. Moved 80% of customer base to EDI, saving over 5000 hours per year in data entry.

- Ran document management project, which eliminated the need to store 500 boxes of financial documents in a secure off-site facility.

- Oversaw ecommerce site development. Site facilitated $2.5 million in revenue in its first year.

These examples contain multiple hooks. We see a candidate who knows how to prioritize and delivers projects within budget and on schedule. Someone who *impacts the business in meaningful ways.* A manager who runs projects that save hours, eliminate paper, and generate revenue. This is what CIO's look for when they hire managers into their departments.

Now to round out your Professional Experience section, think about things you may have done that show leadership and attention to your team's career growth. Examples:

- Instilled formal mentoring program.

- Established program to improve team's soft skills. Sessions included communication, leadership, conflict resolution, and culture building.

- Launched teamwork initiative based on the model outlined in *The Five Dysfunctions of a Team.*

Where to go from Here

By now, you should have at least a rough draft of your resume, but if not, *right now* is a great time to start! Take a few minutes and review the appendixes, which contain some great key words and phrases to help get you off the ground. Use the tips you've learned throughout these chapters. Make your resume interesting and impactful. Get that interview. Land that job.

Even if you're not currently looking for a job, always keep your resume up-to-date, because you never know what might come your way. Keep this book handy and refer to it often. Good luck!

Appendix

Appendix A

Career Summary Phrases

Use this appendix to help with your Career Summary section.

General

- Proficient
- Proven
- Professional
- Exceptional
- Principled
- Who thinks outside the box

- Business savvy
- Respected
- Recognized
- Skilled
- Inspirational
- Creative

Work Ethic

- Diligent
- Highly motivated
- Dedicated
- Self-starter
- Thorough
- Disciplined
- Quickly resolve issues
- Detail oriented
- Work effectively under high-pressure

- Productive
- Hard worker
- Proactive
- Tireless
- Meet deadlines
- Dependable
- Take initiative
- Committed
- Able to work with minimal supervision

Attitude

- Positive attitude
- Team player
- Quick learner
- Bring out the best in my team
- Able to handle surprises
- Always looking for ways to contribute
- Who works hard and also has fun on the job
- Energetic
- Flexible
- Adaptable
- With a good sense of humor
- Stays calm under pressure
- Always ready to learn something new
- Who inspires team members to achieve their potential

Communication

- Coach and mentor others
- Able to interact effectively at all levels in the organization
- With excellent communication skills
- Who communicates clearly and concisely
- Who delivers powerful presentations
- Who gets along well with others
- Comfortable presenting to senior management
- Who communicates openly and effectively
- Communicate confidently with all levels of management
- Who builds a climate of trust

Results

- Who produces a positive impact
- Demonstrates a high level of expertise
- Always looking for ways to drive improvement
- Who effectively sets and achieves objectives
- Rapidly diagnoses root causes and corrects problems
- Who is uniquely qualified
- Who achieves consistently high results
- Able to balance solution, scope, and deadline
- Continuously improves the organization
- Who overcomes barriers and achieves results

Appendix B

List of IT Skills

Use this appendix to help build out your Skills section.

Management Skills

- Project management
- Project portfolio management
- Program management
- Team management
- Personnel management
- Professional services
- Business case development
- IT strategy
- Strategic planning
- Solution delivery
- Delegation
- Proposal writing
- Contract negotiations
- Cross-functional supervision
- Scrum methodology
- Budgeting
- Teambuilding
- Project conceptualization
- Quality assurance
- Business metrics
- Alignment of business and IT
- Vendor management
- Cost center management
- Profit center management
- Mentoring
- Critical thinking
- Leadership
- ROI Analysis
- Delegation
- Agile project management

Business Skills

- Business process design
- Business process Improvement
- Business transformation
- Integration
- Manufacturing strategies
- Make-to-order manufacturing
- Make-to-stock manufacturing
- Warehouse management
- Inventory management
- Supply chain planning
- Supply chain optimization
- Supply chain execution
- Shop floor execution
- Capacity planning
- Transportation planning
- General ledger
- Product costing
- Product cost planning
- Digital marketing
- Benefits realization
- Six Sigma
- Total Quality Management
- Lean Management
- Pricing
- Retail pricing
- Retail assortment planning
- Promotion planning
- Purchasing
- Procurement
- Sales and distribution
- Sales order processing
- Customer service
- Logistics
- Batch management
- Serial numbering
- Serialized products
- Credit management
- Organizational change management

Life Skills

- Critical thinking
- Active listening
- Effective speaking
- Customer service
- Building rapport
- Conversational interviewing
- Negotiation
- Decision making
- Leadership
- Organization
- Creative thinking
- Behavioral interviewing
- Relationship building
- Time management
- Conflict resolution
- Public speaking
- Positive language
- Prioritization
- Effective communication
- Problem solving
- Writing concisely
- Presentation
- Self-motivation
- Persuasive writing
- Motivational speaking
- Mentoring

Technical Skills

- Design
- Database design
- Interface design
- User interface design
- Enhancement design
- Hardware configuration
- Problem diagnosis
- Incident management
- Networking
- GUI design
- Interactive design
- Blueprinting
- Development
- Interface development
- Software development
- Mobile development
- Debugging
- Database platforms
- Data conversion
- Master data management
- Network technologies
- Unified modeling language
- Adobe Dreamweaver
- Adobe Flash
- Illustrator
- Acrobat
- Remedy
- Java, JavaScript
- HTML, XHTML
- CSS
- C++, C#
- IOS / Swift
- SQL, MySQL
- Python
- .Net, Visual Studio
- Unit testing
- Integration testing
- Workflow
- Requirements analysis
- Web content management
- Software installation
- Troubleshooting
- VPN/Remote connectivity
- LAN and Wi-Fi connectivity
- Search engine optimization (SEO)
- Business analytics
- Business Intelligence
- IT security
- IT authorizations
- Training development
- User training
- Technical writing
- Documentation
- Object-oriented development
- Hand-held technologies
- Technical support
- Customer relationship management
- SAP ABAP, SAPscript
- SAP NetWeaver
- SAP Hana
- Hybris
- JIRA
- Hadoop
- MAC OS
- PHP
- Windows
- Linux
- Unix
- Oracle
- Informix

Appendix C

List of Impact Verbs

Use this appendix to help with your Professional Experience section.

Hands-on Impact Verbs

- Identified
- Defined
- Gathered
- Designed
- Modeled
- Customized
- Developed
- Created
- Wrote
- Constructed
- Tested
- Performed
- Installed
- Authored
- Trained
- Conducted
- Repaired
- Corrected
- Collected
- Assessed
- Analyzed
- Prepared
- Evaluated
- Configured
- Set up
- Built
- Coded
- Converted
- Completed
- Deployed
- Upgraded
- Taught
- Delivered
- Diagnosed
- Resolved
- Monitored

Management Impact Verbs

- Implemented
- Managed
- Coordinated
- Responsible for
- Accountable for
- Focused on
- Acted as
- Selected for
- Conducted
- Oversaw
- Drove
- Supervised
- Accomplished
- Applied (methodologies, tools)
- Sponsored
- Assessed
- Launched
- Expanded
- Staffed
- Rolled out
- Carried out
- Completed
- Resolved
- Organized
- Planned
- Led
- Established
- Directed
- Administered
- Mitigated (risk)
- Guided
- Anticipated
- Ensured
- Obtained
- Conceptualized
- Replaced
- Facilitated
- Spearheaded

Improvement Impact Verbs

- Reduced
- Increased
- Realized (benefit)
- Responsible for
- Attained
- Improved
- Optimized
- Exceeded (goals, targets)
- Boosted
- Eliminated
- Standardized
- Enabled
- Gained
- Commended for
- Promoted to (rank or position)
- Strengthened
- Streamlined
- Automated
- Delivered
- Accelerated
- Demonstrated
- Grew
- Maximized
- Simplified
- Expanded
- Achieved
- Drove (improvement, gain)
- Stabilized
- Honored with
- Received (awards or recognition)

Participation Impact Verbs

- Participated in
- Jointly prepared
- Co-developed
- Assisted
- Strengthened
- Learned
- Gained experience with
- Helped
- Worked with

- Supported
- Monitored
- Maintained
- Provided
- Collaborated with
- Reinforced
- Contributed
- Partnered with
- Consulted with

Appendix D –Sample IT Resume

John Smith

(303) 555-1234 | City, State | johnsmith@gmail.com | LinkedIn.com/JohnSmith

Java and Web Developer

Exceptional developer with eight years of IT success. History of building progressively more complex programs across a wide variety of clients in almost every industry. Deep expertise in C++, Java, Visual Basic, and many other programming languages. Energetic, positive, and effective in high-pressure situations.

Skills

✓ GUI design	✓ Database design	✓ IOS / Swift
✓ Mobile development	✓ Interface development	✓ Java, JavaScript
✓ XML	✓ C++, C#	✓ HTML, DHTML
✓ CSS	✓ Adobe Illustrator	✓ Adobe Flash
✓ SQL, MySQL	✓ Visual Studio	✓ Technical writing
✓ Business metrics	✓ Creative thinking	✓ Leadership

Professional Experience

ABC Brands   **1/2014 – Present**
Developer

Developed sales and ecommerce applications for this global leader in sports apparel. Supported 40 sites and over 500,000 customers. Applications primarily coded in Visual C++ and Java.

- Created e-commerce functionality to suggest complimentary products upon checkout. Project increased average order value by 16%.
- Built enhancements to streamline checkout process. Reduced shopping cart abandonment by 22%.
- Co-developed point-of-sale application that processes 25,000 transactions daily. Responsible for complex scenarios such as partial exchanges and returns.

XYZ Consulting   **1/2010 – 12/2013**
Developer

Implemented and maintained web applications for multiple clients. Used Visual Studio, Java, HTML, XHTML, Adobe Illustrator, and Adobe Flash.

- Built web concept from the ground up for midsize electronics company. Site generated $2 million in revenue the first year.
- Designed employee self-service application for automobile component supplier. Application handled payroll and expense reporting for over 1000 users.
- Coded web applications and enhancements for numerous other customers using Java, HTML, and XHTML.

Education

Bachelor of Computer Science, University of California, Los Angeles, 2009. GPA 3.8.

Made in the USA
Monee, IL
23 August 2021